201

Knockout Answers to Tough Interview Questions

The Ultimate Guide to Handling the
New Competency-Based Interview Style

Linda Matias
JCTC, CIC, NCRW

AMACOM

American Management Association

New York • Atlanta • Brussels • Chicago • Mexico City • San Francisco
Shanghai • Tokyo • Toronto • Washington, D.C.

Special discounts on bulk quantities of AMACOM books are
available to corporations, professional associations, and other
organizations. For details, contact Special Sales Department,
AMACOM, a division of American Management Association,
1601 Broadway, New York, NY 10019.
Tel.: 800-250-5308.   Fax: 518-891-2372.
E-mail: specialsls@amanet.org
Website: www.amacombooks.org/go/specialsales
To view all AMACOM titles go to: www.amacombooks.org

*This publication is designed to provide accurate and authoritative information
in regard to the subject matter covered. It is sold with the understanding that
the publisher is not engaged in rendering legal, accounting, or other professional
service. If legal advice or other expert assistance is required, the services of a
competent professional person should be sought.*

Library of Congress Cataloging-in-Publication Data

Matias, Linda.
  201 knockout answers to tough interview questions : the ultimate
guide to handling the new competency-based interview style / Linda Matias.
       p.   cm.
    Includes bibliographical references.
    ISBN-13: 978-0-8144-1500-9
    ISBN-10: 0-8144-1500-8
    1. Employment interviewing.   2. Core competencies.   I. Title.   II. Title:
    Two hundred and one knockout answers to tough interview questions.   III. Title:
    Two hundred one knockout answers to tough interview questions.

    HF5549.5.I6M3178 2010
    650.14'4—dc22

                                                                      2009014411

Printing number

10   9   8   7   6   5   4   3

Contents

Introduction vii

201 Competency-Based Interview Questions at a Glance xi

PART I: THE FUNDAMENTALS 1

Chapter 1: What Are Competency-Based Interviews? 3
    Competency–Based vs. Traditional Interview Questions 3
    Proficiencies That Competency–Based Questions Measure 5
    Industry–Specific Competencies 6

Chapter 2: Preparing for Competency-Based
Interview Questions 23
    Identify and Highlight Your Accomplishments 23
    When You Lack Specific Experience 24
    Industry–Specific Accomplishments 25
    Identify Your Core Competencies 30
    Keep SOAR in Mind 34

Chapter 3: Leverage Your Competency-Based Résumé 36
    Competency–Based Résumé Tips 37
    Accomplishment-Based Information 38
    The Objective or Profile Statement 39
    The Professional Experience Section 41
    Selected Résumé Formats 43

Chapter 4: Why Candidates Do Not Get Hired 47

When Examples Go Wrong 47

A Negative Mind-Set 49

A Potpourri of Other Interview Mistakes 50

Chapter 5: Seven Ways to Stand Out During the Interview 52

Write a Personal Brand Statement 53

Reduce Your Anxiety 54

Improve Your Speaking Voice 55

Be Concise 56

Common Words and Phrases to Avoid 56

Make Specific Statements 58

Script or Outline Your Responses 59

PART II: COMPETENCY-BASED QUESTIONS AND ANSWERS 61

Chapter 6: Competency #1—Individual Responsibility 63

Decisiveness 63

Independence 70

Flexibility 77

Career Goals 85

Chapter 7: Competency #2—Managerial/Leadership Skills 93

Leadership 93

Employee Motivation 100

Ability to Delegate 107

Strategic Planning 114

Chapter 8: Competency #3—Personal Motivation 122

Ambition 122

Initiative 129

Chapter 9: Competency #4—Analytical Skills 137
Problem Solving 137
Attention to Detail 145

Chapter 10: Competency #5—People Skills 153
Team Orientation 154
Customer Service 161
Communications 167

PART III: THE END OF THE INTERVIEW 177

Chapter 11: Closing the Job Interview 179
Some Closing Mistakes 180
The Closing Statement 181

Chapter 12: The Interview Follow-Up 184
Follow-Up Pointers 185
Competency-Based Follow-Up Letters 186

Contributors 197

About the Author 199

Introduction

The job interview. It's a constantly evolving environment. Just when candidates think they have figured it all out, they are exposed to competency-based interview questions (also known as behavioral-style interviews) that leave them clueless as to how to respond.

Competency-based interviews are quickly gaining popularity among hiring professionals as the most effective questioning strategy to identify and hire the right people. But what are competency-based interviews and how do these interviews work? Competency-based interviews are when interviewers focus on core competencies that are essential for success on the job. In addition, behavioral-style interview questions target the candidates' accomplishments, which gives them an opportunity to showcase their successes.

This book presents 201 competency-based interview questions that you are likely to be asked so you will know the best way to answer these questions. This book provides the tips and guidance you need to succeed in today's competitive marketplace. To make it easier to navigate through the book, the information is split into three parts.

Part I: The Fundamentals. Whenever a new interview method, such as the competency-based interview, is introduced, it's normal for applicants to feel insecure. The key is to not let self-doubt get the best of you, lest you run the risk of getting tongue-tied and making a poor impression. Filled with easy-to-grasp concepts and easy-to-follow advice, Part I effectively prepares you to enter this new world of interviewing.

Part II: Competency-Based Questions and Answers. This part of the book is its core. With these 201 interview questions and answers, you will come away with a clear understanding of how to broach this type of questioning strategy. Each answer has three components: situation, action (or observation), and result. The breakdown of competencies, along with the questions and typical answers, provides you with a variety of objectives and sample responses you can use as a guide when preparing for interviews.

Part III: The End of the Interview. The way you manage the end of the interview, and the course you take once the interview is over. can have a significant impact on whether or not you are offered the position. Complete with a post-interview analysis, this section provides scripts on how to close the interview and sample follow-up letters you can tailor to fit your situation.

Key Attributes and Career Values

Key attributes and career values are personal characteristics and work strengths that employers will measure during job interviews. In the body of this book you will learn how to identify your fundamental competencies and shape each to appeal to employers. However, to begin, you can use your current job description to identify your employment-based traits and your basic career values. Here's how to do it:

Step 1. Pull out your job description and jot down your duties and responsibilities.
Step 2. Write down the actions you take to accomplish each duty.
Step 3. Identify the career values and key attributes important to each.

As an example, see Figure I-1. This shows what one person, presently working as a quality assurance manager, came up with when he followed the three steps just described. As you can see, he took his current job description (to create a safe environment, to conduct OSHA meetings, and to file accident reports) and paired those duties with the actions he took to perform those duties and the employer-desired values and key employee attributes inherent in those actions.

Gathering this job information and viewing it in this manner—in terms of key attributes and career values—will provide you with the resources you need to answer the kinds of competency-based questions that have been presented in this book.

Figure I-1

Job Title: <u>Quality Assurance Manager</u>		
Duties and Responsibilities	**Action Steps**	**Career Values/Key Attributes**
1. Create a safe environment	• Coordinate safety inspections to determine weaknesses	Organizational, leadership, and strategic planning skills
	• Prepare reports on corrective actions	Analytical, problem-solving, and written communication skills
2. Conduct OSHA meetings	• Incorporate OSHA standards in training materials	Organizational management, written communication skills, adhere to regulatory compliance
	• Implement logistics and pace training sessions	Time management, project management
	• Train employees	Verbal communication skills, leadership skills
3. File Accident Reports	• Talk to employees regarding accident	Investigative and verbal communication skills
	• Complete workers compensation paperwork	Written communication skills

The Competency-Based Questions

Chapters 6 through 10 present the 201 questions and give sample responses, keyed to the Key Attributes and Career Values described above. As a further aid, I have presented just the questions in the following section—you might see how well you can answer them right now, even before beginning to read this book. Then compare your initial responses with those in the chapters that follow.

In this increasingly competitive world, securing a job position—especially the position that you want and that will advance your career—requires solid communication skills and the ability to answer these tough competency-based questions. With this guide you will be well on your way to getting that job offer. Good luck!

201 Competency-Based Interview Questions at a Glance

Today's employers are likely to ask a variety of competency-based questions of candidates for their job openings. These questions generally cover five different aspects of competency: individual responsibility, managerial and leadership skills, personal motivation, analytical skills, and people skills. Below are typical questions, grouped by the competency being evaluated.

Although these questions feature most prominently in the five chapters of Part II, familiarity with them will be helpful in understanding all the points of this book, beginning with its first chapter. In particular, Chapters 6 through 10 pinpoint the Key Attributes and Career Values for identifying these competencies and show how you can highlight these marketable and transferable skills to greater advantage.

Competency #1: Individual Responsibility

Decisiveness **Interview Questions**

1. There are times when a firm decision must be made quickly, and there are other times when it is prudent to consider all angles before reaching a conclusion. Give an example of a situation when you took time in making a final decision. (p. 65)
2. Rarely do issues arise that are one-dimensional. With that fact in mind, describe a time you handled a situation that had different layers of dimension. (p. 66)

3. Tell me about a time when you encountered competing deadlines and you had to choose one deadline to fall by the wayside in order to meet the others. (p. 66)

4. It is impossible to please every staff member or client. Describe a time when you made an unpopular decision. (p. 67)

5. Recall a time when you were approached to take sides on an issue, but decided to stay neutral. (p. 67)

6. Tell me about a time when you came up with a way to increase output. (p. 67)

7. Describe an occasion when you made a decision that could have had a negative impact on the company if not managed correctly. (p. 68)

8. Give an example of a time when you were surprised by an unexpected situation and had to change course quickly. (p. 68)

9. Recall a time when you used good judgment and logic in solving a problem. (p. 69)

10. Tell me about a time when you thought a problem was resolved, only to find out that you were mistaken. (p. 69)

11. Not all problems have clear-cut solutions. Give an example of a difficult decision you made and your thought process for making it. (p. 70)

12. Summarize a time when you managed a situation characterized by high pressure. (p. 70)

Independence Interview Questions

13. Because not everyone always agrees with every company policy, tell me about a time when you spoke up against a standard procedure. (p. 72)

14. This division is a department of one. The person hired will be required to manage problems on his or her own. Please describe a time when you dealt with a situation without receiving input from staff members. (p. 73)

15. Working in a team environment has its benefits. Likewise, working independently is also rewarding. Provide an example of a time when you were commended for your ability to complete a task on your own. (p. 73)

16. Describe an occasion when you managed a situation that was your supervisor's responsibility. (p. 73)

17. Describe a time when you felt constraints placed on you that worked against completing your job effectively. (p. 74)
18. Give an example of a situation in which you were selected over your peers to complete a project. (p. 74)
19. Tell me about a time when you lacked experience in a specific area and needed to outsource an initiative. (p. 75)
20. Describe an occasion when you were left to your own devices to manage a situation. (p. 75)
21. Tell me about a time when your success was dependent on another's decision. (p. 75)
22. Describe a time when you went against the status quo. (p. 76)
23. Tell me about a time when you managed a situation on your own while simultaneously adjusting to changes over which you had no control. (p. 76)
24. Recall a time when you made an independent decision. (p. 76)

Flexibility Interview Questions

25. Tell me about a time when you had to adjust to a different work environment. (p. 79)
26. Describe an occasion when there was a fundamental change in the way things were done in your workplace. What was your response to it? (p. 79)
27. Recall the last time you felt energized about a project. (p. 80)
28. Give an example of a situation in which you assessed a person's temperament and how that assessment helped the relationship. (p. 80)
29. Tell me about a time when you had to adjust your priorities to meet someone else's higher priority. (p. 81)
30. Describe the culture of your organization and provide an example of how you worked within this culture to achieve a goal. (p. 81)
31. Give an example of a time when your patience was tested. How did you handle it? (p. 81)
32. Describe a time when you were on the verge of completing a task and were asked to abandon the project for another project. (p. 82)
33. Give an example of a situation in which you worked for a company where your flexibility skills were important. (p. 82)

34. Describe a time when you were required to go to work unexpectedly. (p. 83)
35. Tell me about a time when you altered your work pattern in order to complete a task. (p. 83)
36. Recall a situation in which you had to please more than one person at the same time. (p. 83)
37. Describe an occasion when you dealt with an employee whose demeanor was causing a problem. (p. 84)
38. Describe a situation when your work complemented another staff member's objective. (p. 84)
39. Give an example of a time when you offered your resignation. (p. 85)

Career Goals Interview Questions

40. Recall a time when you made a difficult career move. (p. 87)
41. Describe a time when a company you worked for invested in you professionally. (p. 87)
42. Tell me about a time when you accepted a position that you later regretted. (p. 88)
43. Give an example of a situation in which you took specific steps to meet your career goals. (p. 88)
44. Describe a time when you asked management for direct feedback. (p. 88)
45. Sometimes people have to take up opportunities to achieve professional success. Tell me about a time when you took a chance in your career and the result. (p. 89)
46. Describe an occasion when you expanded your knowledge base to further your career. (p. 89)
47. Tell me about a time when you leveraged your past experience to advance your career. (p. 90)
48. Give an example of how you put the company's needs ahead of your career goals. (p. 90)
49. Tell me about a time when you assumed a position or took on a task that was beyond your experience because you knew it would lead to better opportunities. (p. 90)
50. Give me an example of how your first job prepared you for this one. (p. 91)

51. Tell me about the most competitive situation you have experienced and how you handled it. (p. 91)
52. Provide an example of a real-life experience that prepared you for this position. (p. 92)

Competency #2: Managerial / Leadership Skills

Leadership Interview Questions

53. Tell me about a time you reviewed someone else's work to ensure that quality standards were met. (p. 95)
54. Not every employee is easygoing. There are times when an employee will refuse to carry out an order he or she believes is unfair. Please describe such a time and how you resolved the situation. (p. 96)
55. Describe an occasion when you managed a situation that was out of the ordinary for your position. (p. 96)
56. Tell me about a time you implemented an initiative and met resistance from the majority of your staff. (p. 96)
57. Recall a time you were successful as a project leader. (p. 97)
58. Tell me about a time when you fired an employee whom you personally got along with. (p. 97)
59. Describe a time when a subordinate disagreed with a task he or she was given. How did you manage the situation? (p. 98)
60. Describe an occasion when you trained a cross-functional team. (p. 98)
61. Give an example of a time when you took on a leadership role. (p. 98)
62. Tell me about a time when you brought together two departments to work effectively with each other. (p. 99)
63. Describe a time when a staff member did not meet your expectations and what you did about it. (p. 99)
64. Give an example of a situation in which you changed the status quo in order to cultivate leaders. (p. 100)
65. Describe a time when you managed an individual who had excellent hard skills but needed help with his or her soft skills. (p. 100)

Employee Motivation Interview Questions

66. Tell me about an occasion when you increased employee morale. (p. 102)
67. Recall the last time you dealt with low employee productivity. What was the situation and how did you handle it? (p. 103)
68. Give an example of a time when your coaching efforts failed. (p. 103)
69. Describe a time when you had to address a problem with an employee without alienating him or her. (p. 104)
70. Describe a time when you provided one-on-one training support. (p. 104)
71. Give an example of a unique way that you promoted teamwork. (p. 104)
72. Describe the last training workshop you led. (p. 105)
73. Describe a time when you were responsible for making drastic changes in your department while at the same time had to minimize employees' negative reactions. (p. 105)
74. Tell me about a time when you trained an employee to do his or her job better. (p. 106)
75. Describe a time when you realized that a top producer on your team was growing bored with his or her position. What did you do about it? (p. 106)
76. As much as we may try to get along with everyone else, there are occasions when we cannot. Describe a time when you managed an employee with whom you did not see eye-to-eye. (p. 107)
77. We all have outside interests. Tell me about an extracurricular activity you enjoy. Then describe a time when the skills you learned in that activity made you a better professional. (p. 107)

Ability to Delegate Interview Questions

78. Describe a time when you entrusted a subordinate with an activity that he or she did not complete. (p. 109)
79. Tell me about a time when you delegated work to a group. (p. 110)
80. Describe a time when you divided the responsibilities of a task to members of a group. (p. 110)

81. Tell me about a time when you delegated a project to a junior staff member because you realized you had too much on your plate. (p. 110)

82. Recall an occasion when you got bogged down in a task's details instead of giving the job to someone else. (p. 111)

83. Give an example of a time when you delegated a task and, in the middle of the project, the employee asked you to take it over. (p. 111)

84. Describe a time when you assigned a project to an employee and dealt with the reactions of those who were passed over. (p. 112)

85. Tell me about a time when you provided instructions for doing a task and an employee offered a smarter alternative. (p. 112)

86. Give an example of a time when you delegated a task because you did not want to do it yourself. (p. 113)

87. Recall a time when you asked for employee feedback before delegating tasks. (p. 113)

88. Describe an occasion when you divided the functions of a team among its members. (p. 113)

Strategic Planning Interview

89. Tell me about an important event you managed from beginning to end. (p. 116)

90. Give an example of a time when your strategic planning skills came in handy. (p. 116)

91. Describe an occasion when you were charged with planning a company event. (p. 116)

92. Tell me about a time when you partnered with another department to execute a plan. (p. 117)

93. Describe an occasion when using strategic partners benefited the company's bottom line. (p. 117)

94. Describe a scenario when you helped a stagnant idea become a full-fledged plan. (p. 118)

95. Give an example of a problem or situation that needed an immediate, short-term solution. (p. 118)

96. Recall a time when you developed a mission statement. (p. 118)

97. Tell me about a time when your budget ran on a deficit. What were the circumstances? (p. 119)

98. Describe a time when you questioned the direction your employer was taking. What was the result? (p. 119)

99. Give an example of a situation in which you implemented a plan that had long-range implications. (p. 119)

100. Provide an example of your existing (previous) company's weakness and the steps you took to overcome it. (p. 120)

101. Describe a time when your opinion on an operational matter differed from that of management. (p. 120)

102. Tell me about a time when you consulted a client to ensure that a project went smoothly. (p. 121)

103. Describe a time when you worked as part of an integrated team to come up with a plan of action. (p. 121)

Competency #3: Personal Motivation

Ambition Interview Questions

104. Tell me about a time when you set and achieved a goal. (p. 124)

105. Recall a situation when you took a self-starter approach to a project. (p. 125)

106. Describe a time when you chose a course of action that had a significant impact on your career. (p. 125)

107. Describe your most recent achievement and explain how your actions benefited investors. (p. 125)

108. Give an example of a situation in which you discovered a flaw in operations. What did you do about it? (p. 126)

109. Recall a time when your performance on the job led to greater responsibility. (p. 126)

110. Describe a time when you did not know a problem existed until it was brought to your attention. (p. 126)

111. Give an example of an occasion when your job became mundane and what you did to make the time pass more quickly. (p. 127)

112. Tell me about a time when you were proud of your efforts. What were the circumstances? (p. 127)

113. Describe a time when you requested help or assistance on a project or assignment. (p. 128)

114. Give an example of a situation in which you demonstrated your willingness to work hard. (p. 128)

115. Describe an occasion when you made a difficult choice between your personal and your professional life. (p. 128)

116. Tell me about a time you leveraged contacts to meet a business goal. (p. 129)

Initiative **Interview Questions**

117. Recall a time when you were given a set of instructions that you were unable to follow. (p. 131)

118. Give an example of a situation in which you did something that you knew had little chance of success. (p. 131)

119. Describe an occasion when an idea you had was met with enthusiasm by management. (p. 132)

120. Describe a time when you took an active role in a project for which you had little experience. (p. 132)

121. Give me an example of a time you worked for a startup. (p. 132)

122. Recall a life-altering event that impacted your career choices. (p. 133)

123. Tell me about a time when your hard work was rewarded. (p. 133)

124. Give me an example of a time when you took on a task that was not part of your job description. (p. 133)

125. Tell me about a situation that called upon your strongest quality. What was the result? (p. 134)

126. Recall a time when using your initiative was rewarded. (p. 134)

127. Describe an occasion when you created an opportunity for yourself. (p. 134)

128. Describe a time when you prepared for an obstacle in order to prevent it. (p. 135)

129. Describe a time when you were unable to meet management expectations. What did you do about it? (p. 135)

130. Give an example of a situation in which your greatest weakness negatively impacted a relationship or a project you were working on. (p. 136)

131. Recall a time when you invested time or money in developing your career. (p. 136)

Competency #4: Analytical Skills

Problem-Solving Interview Questions

132. Tell me about a time when you disagreed with management's decision. What did you do about it? (p. 139)
133. Recall a time when you discovered a way to improve upon an existing process. (p. 140)
134. Describe a time when you figured out a problem that others had tried to solve but failed. (p. 140)
135. Give me an example about a time when a routine procedure presented a challenge. (p. 141)
136. Describe a time when you stumbled on a problem you did not know existed. (p. 141)
137. Describe a time when you solved a problem using a skill you acquired through professional training. (p. 142)
138. Tell me about an occasion when you solved a problem without using the resources you needed. (p. 142)
139. There are many people applying for this position. Recall the last achievement that demonstrates you are the right candidate for this position. (p. 142)
140. Describe an occasion when you had to go to work sick. What were the circumstances? (p. 143)
141. Give an example of a small project that you executed that had a departmental impact. (p. 143)
142. Describe a time when your analytical skills were put to the test. (p. 143)
143. Everyone's professional career is peppered with successes and failures. Describe a time when you learned from a mistake you had made. (p. 144)
144. Describe a time when you were creative in cutting costs. (p. 144)
145. Give an example of a time when you had a positive effect on a chronic problem. (p. 144)
146. Tell me about a time when you managed more than one project at a time. (p. 145)

Attention to Detail Interview Questions

147. Tell me about a time when you caught a problem before it escalated. (p. 147)

148. Describe a time when your document-management skills benefited your department. (p. 147)

149. Tell me about an occasion when your attention to detail was recognized by management. (p. 148)

150. Describe a time when addressing a minor project detail made a significant difference in the outcome. (p. 148)

151. Recall a time when a thorough evaluation of events was critical to your company's success. (p. 149)

152. Give an example of a problem you solved with an obvious solution that was overlooked by others. (p. 149)

153. Tell me about an occasion when precision was important in your work. (p. 149)

154. Describe a time when the attention you gave to your work led to additional responsibility. (p. 150)

155. Describe an occasion when you worked on a project that had little room for error. (p. 150)

156. Give an example of a time when you went beyond standard operating procedures to ensure that regulatory compliances were met. (p. 150)

157. Our slogan is "Better Quality, Better Entertainment." With that in mind, give an example of a time when you served that slogan in your previous (existing) position. (p. 151)

158. Tell me about a time when you analyzed a situation and found many mistakes had been made. (p. 151)

159. Recall a situation in which you used more than one skill at a time. (p. 151)

160. Give an example of a time when you participated in a team effort to complete a one-of-a-kind project. (p. 152)

Competency #5: People Skills

Team-Oriented **Interview Questions**

161. Tell me about a situation in which you became aware of a serious mistake made by a colleague and what you did about it. (p. 156)

162. Describe an occasion when you believed in your company even when team members had lowered morale. (p. 156)

163. Describe a time when you were assigned a job-related task that you questioned. (p. 156)

164. Tell me about a time when another department's participation in a project depended on your completing a task first. (p. 157)

165. Describe a time when your team's effort did not meet your expectations. (p. 157)

166. Describe an occasion when you took direction from someone who was not your supervisor. (p. 157)

167. Recall a time when you had a difficult co-worker as part of your team. (p. 158)

168. Tell me about a time you worked on a project when your role was not clearly defined. (p. 158)

169. Give an example of a situation in your current (past) position in which you adapted to the team environment. (p. 159)

170. Describe a time you took on a task that was outside the scope of your job description. (p. 159)

171. Describe a time when you worked on a project that was delayed through no fault of your own. How did you manage the situation? (p. 159)

172. Recall a time when you avoided getting involved in office politics. (p. 160)

173. Tell me about a time when you worked with someone who had a delicate ego. (p. 160)

Customer Service Interview Questions

174. Describe the steps you take to ensure a high level of customer satisfaction. (p. 163)

175. Describe a time when existing policies did not solve a customer's problem and the customer took his or her business elsewhere. (p. 163)

176. As much as we may try to keep customers satisfied, there are times when we drop the ball and they are dissatisfied. Describe a time when a customer had a problem with how you managed his or her account. (p. 163)

177. Tell me about your most memorable customer-service experience. What were the circumstances? (p. 164)

178. Recall the last time a client was dissatisfied with your customer service. (p. 164)

179. Describe a position in which you used technology to assist in answering customer inquiries. What was the process? (p. 165)
180. Tell me about a specific instance in which your customer-service skills were praised. (p. 165)
181. Give me an example of an occasion when a customer withheld information you needed to solve a problem. How did you handle it? (p. 165)
182. Describe a time when you believed a system could be improved. What actions did you take? (p. 166)
183. Describe a time when you made a suggestion that improved customer relations. (p. 166)
184. Recall an occasion when you questioned your ability to do your job. (p. 166)

Communication Skills Interview Questions

185. Give an example of a time when you worked with someone who had an accent. (p. 169)
186. Describe an occasion when your communication style got you out of a tight situation. (p. 169)
187. Recall a time when you did not communicate well. What were the results? (p. 170)
188. Describe a situation when you had to tell someone bad news. (p. 170)
189. Tell me about a time when you used your presentation skills to influence a client. (p. 170)
190. Both written and verbal communication skills are vitally important. This position relies heavily on e-mail communication. To help me assess your experience, describe a time when your correspondence was well received. (p. 171)
191. Describe an experience in which you worked with a culturally diverse population. (p. 171)
192. Give me an example of when you managed to break a communications barrier. (p. 171)
193. Tell me about an occasion when you were optimistic while others around you were pessimistic. (p. 172)
194. Describe a time when you were required to write marketing copy. (p. 172)

195. Describe an occasion when you improved communications within your department. (p. 173)
196. Tell me about a time when you strengthened a relationship through training. (p. 173)
197. Give an example of an important document you are required to write. (p. 173)
198. Recall a time when a team member criticized your work in front of others. How did you respond? (p. 174)
199. Describe a time when you were praised for your listening skills. (p. 174)
200. Describe a situation in which you found yourself dealing with someone with whose personality you clashed. How did you handle the situation? What was the outcome? (p. 175)
201. Tell about a time you built rapport quickly with someone under difficult conditions. (p. 175)

Part I

The Fundamentals

Chapter 1

What Are Competency-Based Interviews?

Competency-based interviews, also known as behavioral-style interviews, offer you an opportunity to demonstrate the skills, proficiencies, and abilities you have developed in the course of your career. By answering interview questions that focus on your *actions* in particular workplace situations, you allow interviewers to compare your experience to the requirements of their open positions. This works to your advantage since the likelihood increases that their hiring decisions will be based on your know-how rather than on the interviewer's personal impressions.

Competency-Based vs. Traditional Interview Questions

Traditional interview questions are broad, allowing the candidate to select an example of a work situation that fits the question asked. These traditional types of interview questions are easy to detect because each typically begins with: "How would . . . ," "How can . . . ," "What would . . . ," "What experience . . . ," "What qualifications . . . ," "Can you describe . . . ," "Have you been . . . ".

For example, the traditional question, "How would you describe yourself?" opens the door for you to answer in very general terms. You can choose to provide a short response, such as "I describe myself as hardworking." Or you can go into detail by saying, "Since my employment with ABC Company, I have never missed a day of work. I take pride in providing customers with a top-notch experience." You also could choose to mention your skills in problem resolution, negotiations, or account management. As you can see, with traditional interview questions, your options as a candidate are unlimited, giving you full control over how you answer each question.

On the other hand, competency-based interview questions are specific. They require you to provide examples in response to questions that are essential for the company and the position for which you are interviewing. An example of a competency-based interview question is: "Describe a time you kept your cool when in a stressful situation." In this case, there is no flexibility for you. The interviewer has laid out exactly what he wants to know. Because of this specificity, competency-based questions are more difficult to answer and they require more thoughtful responses.

Competency-style interview questions begin with phrases such as the following: "Tell me about a time when you. . . ," "Give an example of a situation when. . . ," "Describe an occasion . . .," "Describe a time . . . ," "Recall a time . . . ". They may also involve a follow-up question, asking for elaboration of your cited incident; for example, "Describe a time when there was a fundamental change in the way things were done in your workplace. What was your response to the situation?" Interviewers choose this line of questioning to ensure that they receive a well-rounded response from you.

In addition, interviewers may set up a competency-based question with an introductory statement. For example: "There are times when a firm decision must be made quickly, and there are other times when it is prudent to consider all angles before making a decision. Give an example of a situation when you took your time in making a final decision." Beginning a question with a scenario or an affirmation is a conversation tool that interviewers use to ease your anxiety and get you to open up. And that "opening up" allows you to present yourself as an asset to the company.

Proficiencies That Competency-Based Questions Measure

There are five core competencies that are measured during interviews that include these questions. The competencies are transferable from profession to profession and industry to industry and call for particular traits. They include the following:

Competency #1. Individual Responsibility

- Decisiveness
- Independence
- Flexibility
- Career goals

Competency #2. Managerial/Leadership Skills

- Leadership
- Employee motivation
- Ability to delegate
- Strategic planning

Competency #3. Personal Motivation

- Ambition
- Initiative

Competency #4. Analytical Skills

- Problem solving
- Attention to detail

Competency #5. People Skills

- Communications skills
- Teamwork ability
- Customer service awareness

In addition to these core competencies, interviewers seek industry-specific competencies, as noted on the next page. Lastly, you can find additional competencies in current or previous job descriptions, classified ads, performance reviews, and written correspondences. In Chapter 2 you will find examples of each.

Industry-Specific Competencies

To assist you in identifying key words that regularly appear on résumés, in job descriptions, and in interviews, review the following compilation of competencies for a broad range of industries and professions. Choose your profession, or one that is closely related to it, and become acquainted with the competencies that an interviewer may focus on when you seek employment.

Accounting and Finance

accounts payable
accounts receivable
audit controls
bookkeeping
capital budgets
conduct variance analysis
cost–benefit analysis
development of financial models
due diligence
expense analysis
financial audit preparation
financial planning and reporting
financial statement review and research
forecast consolidation
general ledger accounts
liability management
management of due diligence
management of suspense control
month-end reconciliation
preparation of balanced scorecards
preparation of financial presentations
private equity transactions
pro forma business reporting
quickbooks management

Banking

audit controls and reports asset management
branch operations
credit analysis and/or administration
discrepancy resolution
equity financing
equity research analysis
investment management
investment planning and management
loan administration
loan processing
loan underwriting
portfolio management
quality assurance and control documentation
record accuracy verification
regulatory compliance
return-on-equity (ROE)
risk management
secured lending
statistical reporting

Construction

blueprint reading, budgeting, and pro-forma
client relationships and negotiations
code and safety regulations enforcement
contract administration
cost reduction and avoidance
critical path methods (CPMs)
employee performance management
ground-up projects
job scheduling
key program coordination and management
land acquisition
mentoring and guidance
OSHA compliance
preventive maintenance
problem identification and resolution

project estimating and bidding
project life cycle
project planning and scheduling
project specifications
quality control and assurance
risk assessment
statements of work and modifications
structural engineering drawings
team building
turnaround and change leadership
work breakdown structures (WBS)

Customer Service

account analysis and retention
account management
claims processing
client relations
collection of delinquent accounts
complaint resolution
customer compliant handling
customer contact
customer liaison
customer needs assessment
customer retention
customer satisfaction
customer service delivery
data collection and survey
data entry
deliverance of world-class service
e-mail customer support
ensurance of integrity of data
entering orders and change requests or returns and credits
execution of follow-up processes
maintenance of order accuracy
management of billing discrepancies
online chat communication
order fulfillment

order processing
order-to-ship process
persuasive communication
problem resolution
procedure compliance
processing of transactions
proper documentation
purchase order transactions
quality assurance
resolution of customer needs
service negotiations

Education Administration

administrative and board relations
assessment and modification
budget analysis and administration
community involvement and leadership
community resourcing
continuous improvement
crisis intervention
curriculum development
departmental leadership
fiscal management
fund-raising
grant writing
management of school budget
organization and management
performance evaluation
school advocate
school improvement initiatives
special program implementation
staff and community relations
staff training
student enrollment
student support and management
supervision of library services
system implementation
teacher support and management

teacher/staff recruitment
team development

Health Care

case management
clinical operations
confidential record keeping
continuance of care
crisis intervention
critical care services
departmental cost review and reduction/avoidance
evaluation and changes
head steering committee
health-care process integration and redesign
HIPAA administration
holistic patient care
inpatient/outpatient care
JCAHO and OPPE regulatory compliance management
leadership of interdisciplinary teams
managed care
medication disbursement
occupational health
operational analysis
patient advocacy
patient assessment
patient education
patient relations
patient service delivery and optimization
physician relations
quality improvement programs and solutions
regulatory compliance
spearheading ad hoc groups

Hospitality

amenities management
back-of-the-house operations
banquet operations
casino promotion and events

catering sales and operations
concierge service
conference management
cost and labor control
daily operations management
fiscal management
food and beverage operations
food cost controls
front-of-the-house operations
inventory control
maintenance of profitable operations
maintenance of sanitation and cleanliness standards
meeting facilities management
menu planning and pricing
occupancy management
provision of safe/quality food
purchasing
rate negotiations
reception / reservations
room service management
spa and recreation
special project execution
up-sell rooms and value added services
vendor relationships and sourcing
venues and dining/tourist information
VIP guest relations
yield management

Human Resources

administrative processes
advocate of employee interests
annual hour operational plan
applicant tracking and reporting
benefits administration
compensation administration
continuous quality improvement
cultural sensitivity training
development of workforce requirements

diplomacy and discretion
DOT compliant
EEO compliance and reporting
employee assistance program (EAP)
employee training/mentoring/evaluation
executive liaison affairs
FMLA management
hour-performance metrics
initial organization assessment
interview screening and hiring
labor and employment laws
maintenance of confidential employee files
multicultural experience
new-hire orientation
new program orientation
recruitment and selection process
payroll management
performance appraisals
policy and procedure design/implementation
pre-employment assessments
statistics reporting
team building and development
wellness programs

Information Technology

applications development
architecture development
artificial intelligence
assistance configuration
business process optimization
client/server architecture
content development
data acquisitions system
database administration
desktop support
disaster recovery
end-user support
equipment routing

field support
hardware configuration
help desk
industrial automation
inventory control
local area network (LAN)
multiuser interface
network connectivity management
network designer
network planning and optimization
new and emerging technologies
new systems development
performance enhancement
requirements specifications/analysis
server integration
system acquisition
systems administration
systems integration/migration, testing, and troubleshooting
user training and support
virtual private network integration
wide area network (WAN)

Law

alternative disputation resolution
arbitrations management
bankruptcy
business process reengineering
civil and commercial litigation
client requirements assessment and evaluation
court forms preparation
courtroom trial preparation
depositions
discovery
draft and review contracts
due diligence
electronic data discovery solutions
estate administration/planning
ethics board member

exhibition hearing preparation
family law
insurance defense
interdepartmental coordination
judicial affairs
large-scale document review and production
legal advocacy
legal research
legal tasks coordination mediation
litigation discovery process
litigation management
medical and employment records summation
medical malpractice
memoranda communication
multi-sector/industry background
personal injury
RFP responses
senior management relations
senior-level client service delivery
settlement negotiations
solution and methodology formation/delivery
workers compensation

Management and Executive Positions

budget administration
business process engineering
competitive market positioning
continuous process improvement
fiscal management
full-cycle product management
go-to-market launch
margin improvement
market and trend analysis
operations management
policy development
profit and loss management
quality assurance
regulatory compliance

revenue and profit management
shareholder relationship
Six Sigma lean operations
start-up operations
training and development
turnaround management

Manufacturing and Operations Management

best-in-class operations
budget forecast
change management
continuous-improvement processes
contract interpretation and execution
cost avoidance
cost containment
cycle-time reduction
environmental training
fleet maintenance and optimization
implementation of process-improvement methodologies
inventory control
just-in-time (JIT) inventory management
lean manufacturing practices
logistics operations
maintenance of service machine smart data
on-time delivery management
performance matrix implementation
policy development
pre-shipment inspection
procurement productivity improvement
production processes and controls
project management
quality and performance improvement
regulatory compliance
route productivity management
safety processes and training
scheduling of management
supply-chain management
systems integration testing

technical manual creation
union negotiations
warehouse operations processes

Marketing

B2B marketing strategy development
B2C marketing strategy development
brand building and development
competitive market positioning
competitive product positioning
copywriting and taglines
creative direction and leadership
customer and marketing dynamics
direct and channel marketing
competitive market analysis
e-commerce strategy and development
event planning and execution
interactive media
marketing campaign launch
marketing collateral development
online branding strategy
product naming
public relations and advertising
trade show execution

Office Administration

access database management
administrative processes
appointment scheduling
back-end operations
confidential correspondence
data entry functions
executive liaison
file/records management
front-end operations
lean administrative processes
management support

meeting & event planning
office management
policy and procedure management
PowerPoint presentations
process improvement
project management
records management
regulatory reporting
report documentation
travel and meetings scheduling, planning, and coordination
vendor communications
workflow management

Project Management

anti-discrimination laws
budget administration
code and safety compliance
contract negotiations
cradle-to-grave management
determining deliverables
idea generation
lease signing
plan execution and monitoring
procedure development
productivity improvement
project closure
project concepts
project development
project life cycle
project management
project prioritizing
report generation
resident screening
risk management
schedule management
stakeholder management
tenant dispute mediation
tenant relations

Public Relations

brand management
budget management
collateral development
community relations
concept development
corporate sponsorships attainment
grassroots campaigning
internal and external communication
logistic management
media liaison
media placement
press release development
special events coordination
strategic communications plan
tradeshow implementation
vendor selection

Purchasing and Logistics

accredited purchasing practitioner (APP)
bid review
capital acquisitions
certified purchasing manager (CPM)
commodities purchasing
component analysis
contract change order
contract negotiations
cradle-to-grave procurement
fleet cost reduction
identification of high-margin opportunities
just-in-time purchasing
logistics management
monitoring departmental expenditures
multisite operations
order expediting
order and requisitions placement
procurement

quality and cost control
regulatory compliance
requests for proposal
requests for quotation
securing written quotations
specifications compliance
subcontractor negotiations
supplier quality
vendor selection
warehousing and distribution

Retail Management

credit operations
customer management
distribution management
employee training and development
incentive structures
in-store promotions
inventory control
key performance indicators
loss prevention
merchandising
multisite operations
performance management shrinkage
stock management
store operations management
succession planning
talent selection

Sales

account and customer retention
account management
B2B and B2C consultative sales
brand positioning and management
business development
client needs assessment
competitive market positioning

consolidated sales
consultative sales
contract negotiations
customer service delivery
effective prospecting techniques
market expansion
multichannel distribution
national account management
network cultivation
new business development
portfolio management product positioning
public speaking and formal presentations
relationship building
return on investment
sales cycle management
sales forecasting
solutions selling
strategic alliances
strong closing performance
territory management
value added sales
vendor selection and relations
win-win negotiations

Social Work and/or Therapy

at-risk patient assessment
behavior modification planning
case management
client advocacy
community outreach
crisis intervention
discharge and placement planning
facilitating group support meetings
foster care knowledge
group therapy
intake assessment
interdisciplinary team membership

life skills
mental and psychosocial assessment
patient needs identification
progress notes documentation
regulatory compliance
provision of resources
psychosocial assessment
short-term psychotherapy
supportive counseling

Teaching

assessment tools
cognitive strategies
cooperative learning
creating life-long learners
creative lesson planning
curriculum development and delivery
early childhood intervention
guided reading
incorporation of "real-life" lessons
individualized education plans
interactive learning
interdisciplinary reading
literacy balanced approach
mathematics enrichment program
multisensory lessons
parent-teacher conferences
reading strategies
role playing
rubrics
student motivation
student-centered teaching
team teaching method
technology integration
textbook review
thematic units
unit plan development
writer's workshop

Determine your specific competencies, based on your prior work experience, and fit them to the five core competencies listed above. You will then be prepared to give the right kinds of answers to the competency-based questions you'll be asked in your next job interview. The better prepared you are to answer these questions, the more confident you'll be during the interview—with more likely successful results.

Chapter **2**

Preparing for Competency-Based Interview Questions

An interview that includes competency-based questions will run longer than a traditional interview because the interviewer may choose to spend ten to fifteen minutes on each competency, asking you to elaborate or provide more examples. Interviewers may also opt to ask more than one question regarding each competency, so as to get a broader view of your experience and to avoid basing their perceptions on only one response.

So, how do you prepare for these questions? In this chapter I provide some strategies for a variety of personal situations.

Identify and Highlight Your Accomplishments

Recent accomplishments are easy to come up with during an interview because they are fresh in your mind. Yet, to appear competitive and provide diverse examples during the interview, you cannot rely solely on your current or last position as a performance indicator. Dig into your past and view your achievements in different lights; each activity in your history can be an ingredient in a tasty recipe that reveals your rich professional capability. Think about those activities in your past and make a list of them. As a result, you will have ample illustrations to choose from when responding to these questions.

Keep the following in mind as you compile your list:

⊘ *Think small.* Accomplishments come in many forms. If you cannot think of extraordinary examples for every question, that's fine. Mentioning occasions when you received an e-mail acknowledgment for a job well done or a time when you made a small but significant difference in your job performance, will impress interviewers as much as extraordinary examples.

⊘ *Quantify the results.* Increasing productivity or decreasing downtime or lowering overhead are impressive feats to accomplish for a company. Whenever possible provide interviewers with a percentage change or a dollar amount; this quantification will add weight to your responses.

⊘ *Accomplishments are relative.* Although helpful, numbers are not always everything. There is a false rumor among job seekers that accomplishments are limited to numbers. That is not the case, however. Your accomplishments are relative—relative to others with whom you work, relative to your field and position, relative to time and situation. Some accomplishments are subtle but significant. For example, an executive assistant's list of accomplishments could include the implementation of a new filing system, not quantifiable but nevertheless an important contribution to efficiency. The achievement is noteworthy because it demonstrates the assistant's ability to meet or exceed expectations.

When You Lack the Specific Experience

Ideally, your list of achievements will include specific examples. However, some of you will not have had the necessary experience to demonstrate your abilities. Of course, you have the option of simply informing the interviewer that you do not have said experience, but that is not advisable. Chances are, in your background you had some opportunities to accumulate the same skills as the interviewer is seeking, perhaps via a different route. You need to use the opportunity of this question to present your skills as comparable. In these circumstances, you have two viable choices:

Choice 1

Choose an example that closely relates to the question asked.

COMPETENCY—BASED QUESTION: "Describe a time when you were charged with sourcing new vendors for a project."

POSSIBLE RESPONSE: "All the companies I have worked for had first-rate vendors, so sourcing new ones was not needed. However, I did nurture the relationships with existing vendors and was able to renegotiate prices, successfully slashing purchasing costs by ten percent."

Choice 2

Provide a hypothetical example when you can't offer a real example. Answering hypothetically allows you to demonstrate your flexibility and your capacity to handle a situation if it came your way.

COMPETENCY-BASED QUESTION: "Tell me about a time when you received a commendation from management for a job well done."

HYPOTHETICAL RESPONSE: "I cannot recall a specific time when I received a commendation, but, if I may, I'd like to describe my work ethic. For example, recently I volunteered to work overtime and without compensation to develop and implement a bi-weekly innovative education and training seminar for thirty employees. This employee training resulted in an enhanced team environment in which staff members performed at a consistently high level."

When you do not have specific experience to cite, you need to take care in offering a response. Refrain from sounding apologetic, because doing so will only make you look unqualified for the position. Additionally, do not answer a competency-based question hypothetically when you *do* have the hands-on experience the interviewer is seeking.

Industry-Specific Accomplishments

Every industry is unique and presents its own challenges. To prepare answers to competency-based questions that are specific to your industry or profession, career expert Wendy Enelow suggests that you use the following points as a guide for identifying your accomplishments.

Accounting and Finance

It is all about the money! In this field, cite and use the specifics of. . .

- Improvements in revenues, profits, ROI, EBITDA, and other financial measurements
- Design/implementation of cost controls and quantifiable results
- Negotiation of contracts, including dollar amounts, profits, cost savings
- Implementation of automated programs, tools, and technologies to optimize business performance
- Partner relationships with investors, pension plan administrators, board of directors, auditors, and others
- Merger, acquisition, joint venture, and divestiture experience

Administration and Office Management

It is all about organization and efficiency!

- Design/implementation of streamlined work procedures and processes
- Introduction of automated tools, programs, and systems to enhance efficiency
- Internal and external communications responsibilities
- Contributions to improved operations, cost reductions, and overall performance improvements
- Personnel training and development experience, and the success of those employees
- VIP and executive responsibilities and relationships

Customer Service

It is all about customers, clients, patrons, and others!
- Improvements in customer service and customer satisfaction scores
- Top industry rankings for quality of customer service organization
- Contributions to sales growth

- Key account management responsibilities and results
- Introduction of automated customer service technologies and tools
- Reductions in customer service operating and overhead costs

Engineering

It is all about development and improvement!

- Engineering/design of new products and their positive financial impact on the organization
- Engineering/design of new processes and their positive financial impact
- Redesign of existing products and their resulting financial/market/customer impact
- Patents awarded and/or pending
- Integration of advanced technologies to expedite engineering and expand capabilities
- Project planning, management, staffing, leadership, and financial success
- Engineering/design of new products and their positive financial impact on the organization

Executive and General Management

It is all about bottom-line performance!

- Measurable increases in revenues, profits, EBITDA, ROI, and other financial indices
- Leadership of/contributions to strategic planning and long-term business development
- Leadership of/contributions to mergers, acquisitions, joint ventures, and business-building initiatives
- Success in expanding into new markets, new geographic regions, new countries, and more
- Improvements in organizational performance, infrastructure, productivity, yield, and more
- Recruitment and leadership of successful management teams (and their contributions)

Health Care

It is all about quality!

- Positive impact on quality of care and quality of patient outcomes
- Expansion of health care services, programs, and outreach to meet patient needs
- Development of innovative new health care delivery systems, medical procedures, and the like
- Attainment and maintenance of stringent regulatory requirements
- Implementation of advanced health care and health care support technologies
- Reduction in disease incidence and overall health improvement of targeted patient base

Human Resources

It is all about the people and their impact on the organization!

- Success in recruiting personnel and their performance within the organization
- Improvements in traditional employee benefits and reductions in premium costs
- Introduction of innovative employee benefits and incentives (e.g., flex time, on-site day care)
- Expansion of HR information systems and technologies
- Creation of expatriate recruitment, training, employee support, and related programs
- Measurement improvements in manpower and organizational performance/productivity

Law

It is all about distinction!

- Managing prestigious cases and clients
- Breadth of legal experience across multiple legal disciplines
- Demonstrable expertise within one area of legal specialization
- Success in negotiations, arbitrations, mediations, and the courtroom

⊘ Relationships with regulatory, legislative, judicial, and other agencies/organizations

Manufacturing and Production

It is all about yield and output!

⊘ Increases in production yield and output, worker productivity, and other performance measurements
⊘ Improvements in quality performance and award of quality certifications
⊘ Reductions in operating costs and overhead expenses
⊘ Design, set-up, and start-up of new manufacturing facilities and production lines
⊘ Seamless introduction of new products into existing manufacturing plants and favorable financial results
⊘ Implementation of new technologies, robotics, and other automated processes, systems, and equipment

Retail

It is all about product movement and sales performance!

⊘ Increases in revenues, profits, and market share
⊘ Improvements in product movement, from warehouse to retail floor to customer sale
⊘ Distinction for merchandise design and display (including sales results)
⊘ Departmental staffing and management responsibilities, and quantifiable results
⊘ Implementation of POS, interactive selling, online selling, and other automated retail technologies
⊘ Reductions in store operating costs, staffing costs, loss rates, and other expenses

Sales and Marketing

It is all about capturing clients and generating profitable revenues!

⊘ Increases in revenues, profits, and market share
⊘ Individual sales and account achievements

- ⊘ Capture of new key accounts and revenue streams
- ⊘ Sales honors, awards, and percentages over quota
- ⊘ Development of new territories and new markets
- ⊘ Introduction of new products and services (and results)

Teaching

It is all about innovation and student/learner excellence!

- ⊘ Development of new curricula and instructional programs
- ⊘ Development of computerized and Web-based programs and teaching/learning tools
- ⊘ Committee memberships, student activities, and special projects
- ⊘ Management responsibilities for programs, budgets, resources, personnel, and more
- ⊘ Experience in training and developing other teaching staff
- ⊘ Measurement of student/learner performance and achievement

Technology

It is all about technology innovation and advances!

- ⊘ Development of new technologies and their organization/operational/market impact
- ⊘ Involvement in emerging e-commerce, e-learning, Web 2.0, telecommunications, and other technologies
- ⊘ Financial benefits of technology (e.g., revenue gains, cost reductions, productivity improvements)
- ⊘ Patent awarded and/or pending
- ⊘ Success in systems migration, conversion, integration, and more
- ⊘ Domestic and international technology transfer programs and ventures

Identify Your Core Competencies

The competencies that are important in your profession or industry can be found in its job descriptions; performance reviews; letters of appraisal from managers, workers, vendors, or business associates; trade publications; and, of course, from your intimate knowledge of the workings of your profession.

It's important that you have fluency in the language of your profession or industry and that you can speak comfortably with the interviewer about these competencies. Review the following sources of information on core competencies and write them down for easy reference.

⊘ *Job Descriptions and Classified Ads.* Core competencies are listed in job descriptions. For all your past jobs, read the description of your duties and extract the core skills and abilities required to execute those duties and responsibilities. Then you can focus your interview preparation on these proficiencies for maximum effectiveness. Job descriptions and classified ads are one and the same. Both describe the hiring organization and outline the position requirements. Figure 2-1 shows a sample job description, that can also serve as a classified ad, for a customer service representative; notice how it lists the duties and responsibilities as well as the required knowledge, skills, and abilities. For your reference, I've underlined the core competencies.

⊘ *Performance Reviews.* Performance reviews involve evaluation of employees' skills and abilities. The appraisal form used for these evaluations usually lists the proficiencies involved and you can draw from this source when preparing your list of core competencies. Figure 2-2 shows

Figure 2-1 ⌁

Job Title: Customer Service Representative

Purpose: Responsible for providing top-flight quality service to customers

Primary Job Duties and Responsibilities:
• <u>Courteous,</u> hands-on contact with customers
• <u>Strong data entry skills</u>
• Processes customer payments into QuickBooks
• Correct billing errors or discrepancies.
• <u>Troubleshoot</u> customer inquiries and resolve discrepancies

Knowledge/Skills/Abilities:
• Must be able to <u>work overtime</u> when needed
• Good verbal, <u>written, and interpersonal communications</u>
• Accurately <u>follow instructions and company policies</u>

---

a blank performance appraisal form, with the core competencies high-lighted in boldface type. (The form also has blank spaces where the manager or evaluator fills in his appraisal results and where the employee can add his reactions to the evaluation—for this exercise, just ignore those portions of the form.)

Figure 2-2

PERFORMANCE APPRAISAL FORM

Employee Name _____   Manager Name _____
Position Title   _____   Evaluation Period _____
Department   _____

EVALUATION CRITERIA

Exceeds Expectations (E)   Performance **consistently exceeds** acceptable standards of performance for this position.

Meets Expectations (M)   Performance **consistently meets** acceptable standards of performance for this position.

Needs Improvement (NI)   Performance **does not completely meet acceptable** standards of performance for this position.

CORE COMPETENCIES	E	M	NI
1. **Job Knowledge**: Demonstrates a thorough knowledge and understanding of the position. Actively maintains current to enhance job knowledge and skills.	☐	☐	☐
2. **Leadership**: Exhibits the highest standards of professional skills to complete goals and objectives. Accepts accountability for progress in area of responsibility.	☐	☐	☐
3. **Communication**: Effectively provides communication in a professional, clear, and accurate manner. Accepts constructive feedback and listens attentively.	☐	☐	☐
4. **Resource Management**: Effectively utilizes the departmental and organizational resources. Demonstrates time management and fiscal responsibility.	☐	☐	☐
5. **Quality of Work**: Achieves an acceptable level of productivity in a timely and accurate manner. Overcomes challenges and barriers to accomplish performance objectives.	☐	☐	☐
6. **Collaboration**: Works cooperatively with others and promotes a positive team environment.	☐	☐	☐
7. **Community Relations**: Effectively supports the organization's mission and strategic plan. Involvement in organizational events, committees, and special projects.	☐	☐	☐
8. **Professional Development**: Demonstrates commitment to professional improvement. Attends professionally related seminars and pursues learning opportunities.	☐	☐	☐
Overall Performance Rating: Below summarize the employee's job performance and provide specific examples.	☐	☐	☐

List the objectives, goals, and professional development activities for the next performance appraisal year.

Employee's Name   **Employee's Signature**   **Date**

Manager's Name   **Manager's Signature**   **Date**

Note: Signature does not necessarily indicate agreement with the performance appraisal results. The signature indicates only that the performance appraisal was discussed with the employee.

EMPLOYEE COMMENTS

Submitted by Barb Matias

⊘ *Written Correspondence.* Letters and e-mail correspondence that you have written on the job usually contain statements that reflect the core competencies of the position. Scour your correspondence for such examples and add those skills to your list of core competencies. Figure 2-3 is an example of an e-mail message that reflects core competencies that are required for a purchasing position.

Figure 2-3

Terry:

I received the shipment. Thank you for making sure it arrived on time, and for your patience in answering my questions along the way. I'll keep you in mind the next time my office supply runs low.

Sincerely,
Michael Gilmore
Purchasing Agent
www.websitename.com
(954) 555-1111

Keep SOAR in Mind

When answering competency-based questions, think SOAR: Situation or Obstacle, Actions, Result. That is, in framing your response, you need to concentrate on the situation or obstacle, the actions you took to implement a solution, and the results you achieved. But, let's look at each of these steps.

SITUATION OR OBSTACLE: To provide context for the interviewer, begin your response with background information. Depending on the importance of the setup, you do not have to provide too much information—just enough to give the interviewer a feel for the situation (circumstances) or obstacle (impediment).

ACTION: Focus your response on the process you undertook to complete the project or carry out your responsibility.

RESULT: Close your answer with the results of your actions, casting them in a positive light.

This recommendation does not mean that all of your responses have to sound exactly the same. But by using the SOAR technique as a general guideline, you'll be able to keep your answers on target. Once you have assembled a list of your competencies and accomplishments, you can plug the right ones into your answers to the interviewer's competency-based questions.

Leverage Your Competency-Based Résumé

The appearance and content of your résumé play an important part in the interview process. Interviewers look for the core competencies to be highlighted on your résumé as a gauge of your suitability for their positions. When you are able to call attention on your résumé to your hands-on knowledge, you answer, at least in part, some of the interviewer's competency-based questions. To begin, the more competencies you target on the résumé, the better your chances of being invited to that interview. Then, during the interview, the interviewer will direct her questions to the information you provided on the résumé. This works to your advantage, because you get the opportunity to elaborate on those competencies, describing the scenarios that provide the best examples.

In this chapter, you will find tips to consider in preparing your résumé, examples of accomplishment-based questions you are likely to be asked, advice on writing a résumé introduction, and suggestions for preparing the professional experience section of the résumé so it focuses on your competencies. Also, you will find here sample résumés you can use as a guide when developing your own résumé.

Competency-Based Résumé Tips

The purpose of a résumé is not to land you a job but, rather, to get you in the door for an interview. This concept is important because it is integral to the résumé-preparation process. When you feel compelled to include unrelated experience or to clutter a résumé with irrelevant facts, think twice. Do not fill the page with empty sentences and boring details. Instead, prioritize your accomplishments and identify pertinent core competencies that relate to your new job search.

Keep in mind the following résumé-preparation advice:

☑ *Strategize.* Begin the résumé-writing process with the end result in mind. Before you commit words to paper, think about the core competencies that will entice interviewers to call you.

☑ *Focus.* Avoid Jack-of-all-trades résumés. Job descriptions are specific in naming the qualifications and competencies needed for the open position. A résumé that displays more than one career objective won't get you in the door. Let's face it: interviewers are not seeking a combination hairdresser/janitor/customer service representative.

You may hesitate to write a specific résumé because you want the reader to know everything about you—just in case a position opens up that you are semi-qualified for. Unfortunately, this strategy almost always backfires. If you send a résumé that lacks focus, hiring managers will assume you are unfocused, ready to accept any job that comes along. In the meantime, your competition is submitting focused résumés that speak to the competencies that the organization seeks.

It is okay to have more than one focus—most job seekers do. However, if this is your situation, you need more than one résumé! There is no way around this. In order to get noticed, your résumé has to outline the competencies for the particular position you are applying for. If you are applying for two different types of positions, you need to have two different résumés, each tailor-made for the position.

☑ *Be distinctive.* Avoid résumé templates. The majority of résumés out there are formatted with templates, and the result is that they have the same look and feel, making it difficult to differentiate between candidates. When searching for a job, the last thing you want to be is an ordinary, run-of-the-mill applicant.

A distinctive résumé format not only makes you stand out from the crowd but also makes you look more qualified and organized. In truth, how your résumé looks is as important as how it reads. Later on, you'll get the opportunity to see different formatting ideas.

✓ *Be relevant.* Because most hiring managers aren't interested in outdated accomplishments or competencies, your résumé should focus on your last ten to fifteen years of employment. In addition, leave out jobs that are not relevant to the position you are applying for. Eliminating old and irrelevant jobs will leave more room on the page to highlight your career objectives and applicable strengths.

Accomplishment-Based Information

Though you may share a job title with many other people, your accomplishments and how you carry out your responsibilities are what distinguishes you from other qualified candidates. Therefore, you should focus your résumé on not only what you did but also how well you did it. Remember, your résumé is your way to market your strengths on paper, so show a significant difference from the others by including some "talking points."

To assist you in determining these résumé "talking points," below are some points to address:

✓ *Measurable Accomplishments.* Write down ways that you saved the company money. Include information such as the circumstances and the percentage saved. Note the special projects you participated in and the outcomes—describe your role in making the projects successful. Recall times when you resolved a major problem with little investment. Take note of the times you exceeded accepted standards for quality or quantity. Write down a time when you were approached by management to train team members on departmental policies and procedures. Outline changes you spearheaded and each that positively impacted the organization.

✓ *Notable Mentions.* Describe the greatest effort you put into your work. List the awards you won (i.e., President's Club) and the commendations you received (i.e., letter from management for a job well done). What are the top three accomplishments you are most proud of for each position? Include some positive quotations from your annual performance reviews. Identify the areas in which you ranked highest on your annual performance reviews.

✓ *Productivity Accomplishments.* Note any efficiency improvements that you implemented or initiated. Give examples of when you took risks to achieve particular goals. What were the outcomes? Were there times when you identified the need for a program, plan, or service?

✓ *Extras.* Compare your achievements to those of your peers. What are the toughest challenges you faced in the work environment? Did you serve on special committees? Were you ever selected to participate in a special training program?

The Objective or Profile Statement

Each reader who picks up your résumé will make a quick decision as to whether to read it carefully or give it an eight-second scan. Therefore, the top one-third of your résumé should be a powerful statement that sums who you are, that encapsulates your professional experience, and homes in on your core competencies. This is the Objective, or Profile, Statement.

So, instead of writing something weak like, "Seeking a challenging position where there is room for growth," compose a strong statement that incorporates your core competencies for the line of work you are in. Figures 3-1, 3-2, and 3-3 are examples of powerful Objective Statements.

As you can see from the examples, there are several ways to compose a solid opening statement. Figure 3-1 introduces the relevant proficiencies in paragraph form. Figure 3-2 offers the core competencies in a bulleted

Figure 3-1

PETER MENDEZ

836 Main Street   (631) 555-8643
Melville, NY 11747   mendez@email.com

COMMERCIAL OPERATIONS

Accomplished, outcome-driven executive with upper-level management background and year-over-year success in building organizations, integrating businesses, and delivering exceptional results for world-renowned companies. Expertise in developing strategies for multiple product lines, motivating cross-cultural teams to exceed expectations, and creating a culture of success under a variety of conditions.

Figure 3-2

REBECCA SCHWARTZ
465 Park Place
Marietta, GA 30066
(770) 555-9522
schwartz@email.com

Summary of Qualifications

Expertise in developing and implementing strategic plans to meet immediate and long-term goals. Strong trainer, mentor, and leader of cross-functional teams, including technical, service, and administrative personnel. Continually seeks new ways to enhance product offerings, enhance the user's online experience, and achieve the highest possible profit margins. Skilled in forecasting new business opportunities and analyzing complex business situations.

<u>**Knowledge & Skill Areas:**</u>

* Start-Up Business Expansion
* Employee/Team Leadership
* Product Branding/Positioning

* E-Commerce Strategy Planning
* New Sales Channel Integration
* Mergers & Acquisitions Management

Figure 3-3

Tracey Bitler
37 Coal Mine Drive • Wauwatosa, WI 53226
traceybitler@email.com • (414) 555-8209

Systems / Network Technician

New & Emerging Technologies—Testing & Troubleshooting—Network Upgrades
User Training & Support Tools—Disaster Recovery Planning—Problem Identification

Offering Advanced Skills and Record of Consistent, High-Quality Performance in Systems/Network Installation, Configuration, Upgrade, and Migration

ACTIVITIES:
Quality-focused IT professional with 10+ years of experience as systems technician and software/hardware support specialist. Proven ability to create and deliver solutions that meet corporate objectives tied to business and technology performance. Comfortable operating in a wide range of platforms and environments. Effective communicator, able to explain complex processes in easy-to-understand terms for end users. Skilled in proactive identification and resolution of critical systems/network issues.

TECHNOLOGY SUMMARY:

SOFTWARE:	Windows 3x/9x/NT/2000/XP, Microsoft Office 97/2000/XP Pro, GHOST, Remotely Anywhere, WinFax Pro, Laplink Pro, Norton Anti Virus, McAfee Anti Virus, Drive Copy, Remote Desktop, PCAnywhere, VNC, NetMeeting, Clarify, Remedy, CRT (telnet client)
HARDWARE:	IBM-compatible PCs, workstations, Ethernet & Token Ring Protocols, Mother Boards, Video & Sound Cards, Monitors, CD-ROM Drives, Memory Chips, IDE/EIDE/SCSI Hard Drives & other devices, SCSI Controller Cards, Tape Backup Drives, Optical Drives, Optical Scanners, Printers, Firewalls, Wireless Controllers, Wireless Access Points, Mobile Handhelds, BarcodeScanners

list after the introduction. Figure 3-3 integrates the competencies into a statement that also mentions the proficiencies and concludes with mention of hard skills.

The Professional Experience Section

Picture a desk piled high with hundreds of résumés. These résumés were submitted by people who want the same job as you are applying for and they are just as qualified as you are. The person working his way through this stack of résumés will need some pretty compelling information to put your résumé on the "call for appointment" pile. You can provide this compelling information in your Professional Experience section when it focuses on the core competencies being sought. Figures 3-4, 3-5, and 3-6 have examples of solid and effective Professional Experience résumé sections.

As with the Objective Statement, there are several ways you can present the picture of your prior experience. Figure 3-4 uses a bulleted list, which, after the statement of company and title, has focused, bulleted statements that stress core competencies and accomplishments. Figure 3-5 highlights the competencies by pairing them with responsibilities, using a two-column format. Figure 3-6 applies a case study approach, with two examples highlighting the challenges and results.

Figure 3-4

PROFESSIONAL EXPERIENCE

Vice President of Construction
USA Construction Inc., New York, NY (2004 – Present)

– **Achieved 100% on-time completion and safety rate on projects that ranged up to $5 million.** Overcame numerous logistical, scheduling, and personnel challenges (harsh and hostile environments, constant turnover, bottlenecks) to meet and exceed objectives.

– **Created comprehensive training programs for department employees that led to improved team** capabilities and shorter learning curves for new staff. Ensured 100% employee participation in training.

– **Function as Senior Manager for CAD, Survey, Engineering, and Construction departments with** 85 total employees. Work with cross-functional teams (clients and employers) to resolve issues and drive successful project completion.

Figure 3-5

PROFESSIONAL EXPERIENCE

UNIVERSITY HOSPITAL – Philadelphia, PA (2006–Present)
Management Engineer

Conducted operational analyses for Clinical Labs, Health Policy & Clinical Outcomes, Nursing, Outpatient Testing, Radiology, SFD, and other areas to achieve departmental objectives. Led quality improvement teams in several areas, including Women & Children's Programs and SFD; recommended improvements to Infection Control procedures. Worked closely with hospital team members to achieve JCAHO goals.

Key Contributions and Achievements:

Team Leadership	• Led interdisciplinary team in implementing changes in rounding times, lab testing, and ancillary services within the Women & Children's division, bringing patient satisfaction from 88% to 98%.
Cost-Contain Measures	• Decreased unused Operating Room supplies by 38% and eliminated associated SPD overtime costs.
Workflow Prioritization	• Captured $70,000 in staffing cost savings by documenting workflow, identifying significant areas of nonproductive time, and implementing cross-training/reallocation strategies that enabled 2nd stress test room.

Figure 3-6

AGENCY INC. — Atlanta, GA — 2000–Present

**Senior Vice President; Director of Market Intelligence
Vice President; Group Brand Director**

In charge of developing and managing brand strategy/positioning and marketing communications for portfolio of high-tech B2B and B2C clients. Directed and contributed to series of key wins and client programs that included the following:

A summary of various projects and achievements throughout this tenure includes the following:

- Garrison Patient Protection—Conducted research and interviews with physicians, nurses, hospital administrators, and Garrison executives to determine market's interest in patient safety programs. Worked with client to create matrix outlining holistic approach to patient safety.
  - **Result: Drove the launch of the Patient Protection Matrix and supporting messages that are currently used in the company's major sales presentations.**

- FaxMerge, Identity Theft Protection—Conducted online qualitative survey to determine reasons for consumers' presumed apathy regarding identity theft. Developed messages that convinced consumers they were not protecting themselves fully from theft.
  - **Result: Facilitated 39% higher return-on-investment for FaxMerge through new messages.**

Selected Résumé Formats

There are three standard résumé formats: chronological, functional, and hybrid. Figures 3-7, 3-8, and 3-9 offer examples of each format. To determine the appropriate format for you, consider the assets of each:

⊘ *Chronological Résumé.* Professional experience and education are summarized in reverse chronological order. This format is best for those with a stable, solid career progression.

⊘ *Functional Résumé.* Strengths are categorized in a core competencies section and the professional experience appears after that, in chronological order. Career changers, job hoppers, and those returning to the workforce after an extended leave will find the functional format serves them well.

⊘ *Hybrid Résumé.* A combination of the chronological and functional formats, this type showcases the core competencies under a heading such as "Selected Achievements" and the Professional Experience section has items listed chronologically.

The importance of your résumé to the interview process cannot be overstated. A strong, compelling résumé, with easily identifiable core competencies and accomplishments highlighted, will help you get interviews, which is your number-one goal. It can also help you steer the interviewer's competency-based questions in a direction where you are most comfortable discussing those work scenarios and experiences.

Figure 3-7

PATRICIA SCHAFER

36 East 74th Street ▪ New York, NY 10022
212-555-5555 ▪ email@email.com

INTERNATIONAL BUSINESS DEVELOPMENT PROFILE

**International Business Achievements   /   Global Account Management
Extensive Experience in European Markets / Fluent in French, Spanish, & English**

Over 10 years of experience in international sales/marketing functions and proven track record of building high net worth accounts in global markets. Demonstrated strengths in client relationship development, cultural/ethnic perspective, and task management across multiple functions, including Sales, Purchasing, Marketing, and Finance. Well versed in international business practices and protocol. MBA degree.

Core Competencies:

▪ Global Business Strategies	▪ New Market Development	▪ International Business Protocol
▪ Team Building & Leadership	▪ Regulatory Compliance Issues	▪ Key/Large Account Retention
▪ Strategic Partnerships/Allies	▪ Cross-Cultural Communications	▪ Public Speaking/Presentations
▪ Global Project Management	▪ New Program Implementation	▪ Competitive Market Analysis

---

PROFESSIONAL EXPERIENCE

HIGH IMPACT EXPORTS
Executive Director / Consultant (2005–Present)

Teamed with President of high-volume import/export company in carrying out broad range of functions, including accounting and financial management, global marketing, and operations. Cemented company's reputation as reliable source of large-scale branded product inventories for largest worldwide retailers.

Selected Accomplishments:

❑ **Increased profitability 20% through variety of strategies,** including reducing cost of inventory (improved analysis and purchasing), increasing selling price, decreasing debit notes from 10% to under 1%, shortening delivery times, and raising customer satisfaction levels.

❑ **Secured value-added, long-term relationships with global retailers** in Belgium, France, Spain, Italy, and Portugal through in-person meetings and market studies.

❑ **Identified accounting errors for 5th largest worldwide retailer** that represented 2% of annual sales. Discovered $90,000 in fraud-related errors and decreased operational costs $40,000.

CONTINENTIAL INCORPORATED
Account Executive (2003–2005)

In charge of establishing, servicing, and managing relationships with clients from financial, business, scientific, artistic, and political fields spanning 55 different countries. Identified target market and created solutions for expanding account base. Delivered presentations for peers and new employees for motivational purposes.

Selected Accomplishments:

❑ **Earned company and industry production awards** based on high production levels, with average case size at 300% of company's and industry's averages. Upheld persistency ratio above 98% and lapse rate under 1%.

❑ **Built excellent relationships with high net worth clients,** consistently maintaining near-100% retention. Leveraged multicultural understanding to communicate with and address clients' needs.

EDUCATION & CREDENTIALS

Masters of Business Administration, Columbia University Business School, New York

---

Figure 3-8

BRENDA HAMILTON

59 Circle Way • Parkland, FL 33067 • Phone: (954) 555-1212 • Email: hamilton@email.com

---

MARKETING & BUSINESS DEVELOPMENT EXECUTIVE

Cross-Functional Leadership & Direction / Business Process Analysis & Reengineering
Time, Personnel & Resource Optimization / Customer Relationships & Needs Fulfillment
Account Growth & Retention /Consultative Selling Strategies / Territory & Market Expansion

Results-driven, dynamic sales leader with advanced skills and portfolio of record-breaking sales performance in national markets. Effective in assembling, training developing, and supervising cross-functional teams. Subject matter expertise in workers compensation risk management and employee welfare-benefit programs. Able to engineer turnarounds for under-performing units and lead start-up operations to fast-track growth.

CORE COMPETENCIES

STRATEGIC BUSINESS PLANNING & EXECUTION

* Established new business unit within the company, resulting in over $750 million in new business payroll production.

* Designed, developed, and implemented Sales Assist Program, leading to 20% increase in sales production as a direct result.

TEAM BUILDING & LEADERSHIP

* Led team of 12 regional managers in optimizing sales process for larger accounts, reducing acquisition by 35%.

* Assembled cross-functional teams that increased closing rate from 3% to 20%; created mentoring program and reduced turnover of sales force to 10%.

* Earned recognition for building cross-functional team that created 1st on-site service personnel into client location, leading to 200% increase in client retention.

TOP PRODUCER

* Achieved position as Five Million Dollar Club Member in 1997 and One Million Dollar Club Member in 2003–2008 as Business Development Manager. Developed and implemented branch mentor program that resulted in Top 5 finish for plan in 1996.

* Reached top 1% in small group business sales for 2006 and top 5% in annuity sales for 2007.

PROFESSIONAL HISTORY

Director, Major Accounts, Bradsfords Incorporated, Bradenton, FL 2003–Present
Market Manager, Retail Express, Bradenton, FL 2000–2002
Business Development Manager, Staff Leasing Incorporated, Parkland, FL 1995–2000

EDUCATION

Bachelor of Arts in Business Administration
AMERICAN COLLEGE, Fort Lauderdale, FL

Figure 3-9

MONICA LOPEZ

4857 Red Robin Street • Stamford, CT 06901• 203-555-1212 • Email: monica.lopez@email.com

---

FUNDRAISING & PROGRAM MANAGEMENT PROFESSIONAL

Highly creative, results-proven management professional with entrepreneurial drive/vision and 10+ years of experience in capturing revenues and support for non-profit organizations. Skilled in building relationships and securing funding within broad range of fields, including health care, education, arts, and human services fields. Familiar with planned giving options and experience with directing volunteers to achieve institutions' needs in advocacy and fundraising.

AREAS OF EXPERTISE

- Grantsmanship, Fundraising & Development
- Government, Foundation & Corporate Grants
- Strategic Partnership & Relationship Building
- Program Development/Implementation

- Prospecting & Lead Generation
- Presentations & Public Speaking
- Research Data Collection & Analysis
- Deadline & Client Commitments

FUNDRAISING LEADERSHIP EXPERIENCE

- **Fundraising** – Secured $1M in 3 years from foundation, corporate, and government grants for United Cerebral Palsy, including funding for innovative projects in health care, education, technology, and the arts. Identified appropriate prospects, created fundraising strategies, and directed activities of proposal development teams.

- **Partnership Building** – Formed strong, sustainable relationships with community organizations, academic medical centers, government agencies, and educational partners to develop and deliver innovative programs that increased agency's visibility. Saved $1000+ in annual consultant fees through cultivated relationships and strategic partnerships.

- **Grant Writing & Proposal Development** – Gained proficiency in various forms of writing/ghost writing including grant writing and proposal development; efforts generated multimillion-dollar grants.

- **Gift/Donor Identification & Cultivation** – Track record of success in achieving fundraising goals and stewardship objectives, securing operating and capital/institutional gifts that range from $25,000 to $10 million.

PROFESSIONAL EXPERIENCE

Director, Grants Development Program – Charitable Events Incorporated, New York, NY   **1998 to Present**

Recruited by Chief Development Officer to provide leadership and drive growth for the Development Department's foundation, corporate, and government grants program. Manage proposal teams and collaborate with executive team to develop solicitation plans for government, foundation, and corporate grants that would fund organization's top-priority programs. Create and revamp marketing pieces, including fact sheets, brochures, and conference programs.

Impact: Orchestrated turnaround for grants program from declining to fast-growth mode, capturing $1 million in grants over a 3-year period. Recognized as key figure in development of special projects for medical and health care, the arts, education, and human services areas.

- Produced/funded award-winning video on breast health for women with disabilities. Designed, developed, and funded innovative 2-year health education program for individuals with disabilities, garnering $350,000 grant.

- Enhanced projects' funding feasibility by assisting team in conceptualizing and articulating ideas. Designed evaluation research framework to spur progress for funded projects.

- Generated 2x increase in individual donor base with direct mail, telecampaign, cultivation, events, and face-to-face direct solicitation strategies. Conceived/launched high-end "President's Council" donor program and grew "Young Membership" (20-something/30-something) donor program.

EDUCATION

B.A., Magna Cum Laude—Williams College (MA); *PBK*, highest honors in English

---

Chapter 4

Why Candidates Do Not Get Hired

It is often hard to determine the exact reason an interviewer does not extend a job offer. Sometimes even the interviewer cannot pinpoint the basis for a negative decision—simply a gut feeling. But in other cases, the interviewer can cite concrete examples of why things went wrong. You, as the candidate, may not be able to recognize these blunders, so you remain in the dark as to why you were not hired. That's not so good, especially as you want to become employed.

With interviewers' fickleness always in play, it is paramount that you effectively manage the aspects of the interview over which you have control. This chapter provides an overview of controllable gaffes you need to be aware of, lest they cost you that job.

When Examples Go Wrong

Your success in answering competency-based answers is rooted in the quality of examples you offer. In truth, the weaker your response, the better the chances of leaving the interviewer with a negative impression. So, all the stories you provide should focus on the hands-on knowledge you acquired. And all the work experiences should point to a steady development of core competencies.

When answering competency-based questions, avoid mistakes by following these rules:

⊘ *Provide examples.* Ideally, you ought to be able to gather your thoughts without hesitation; however, there may be times when you are not quick on your feet or your mind goes blank. A knee-jerk response often takes either of two forms.

First, you may feel inclined to make a defensive comment, such as the following real-life example: "I do not understand why you are asking such questions. I have the qualifications for the job. But I am not good at interviews." That possibly is the case; nevertheless, an interviewer will not take your word for it and will expect you to demonstrate your capability.

Second, making an obnoxious comment surely will eliminate your candidacy, as will unknowingly making rude facial expressions, such as rolling your eyes. Needless to say, obvious negative reactions tremendously decrease your chances of being hired.

So, when you find you are unable to answer a question or provide a hypothetical scenario, simply come clean by stating: "At the moment I cannot think of an example. Is it possible to move on to the next question?" This situation is not ideal, and should be used rarely, but it's better than insulting the interviewer.

⊘ *Offer details.* When interviewers ask competency-based questions, they want specifics. Failing to provide those specifics will lead the interviewers to conclude that you do not have the right experience for the job.

⊘ *Vary your examples.* Using examples that always contain the same facts, situations, gender, or age group is a warning sign that you do not have a range of experience or can deal with different personalities. To avoid being pigeonholed, provide diverse examples that reflect an array of situations and personalities.

⊘ *Limit your examples.* Depending on the number of years constituting your work experience, you may have many examples to offer. If this is the case, avoid providing too many illustrations, lest you overwhelm the interviewer. To narrow down your choices, stick with the most recent examples.

⊘ *Provide relevant examples.* Answer the questions asked, not the ones you thought you heard. For example, when asked, "Tell me about a time when you acted as a leader," you may be tempted to say, "I am not ready to manage people." However, though this may be accurate, you should provide the information that was requested, not your impression of the question.

Remember, in this example, the interviewer did not ask if the interviewee had experience as a manager but, rather, what his experience was as a leader. A leader comes in many forms. Being in charge of a department is one example of being a leader, but so is taking charge of a team project. You need to focus your response on the experience, not your shortcomings or seeming lack of direct experience. You don't want to leave the interviewer with a negative impression.

A Negative Mind-Set

If you have a downbeat attitude regarding the job search, that attitude seeps into your interviews and minimizes your appeal. Before the interview, make a conscious decision to think positively, no matter what direction the meeting takes.

Your mind-set or attitude shows up in a number of ways. For example, appearing to give up in the middle of the interview will show you as weak, a quitter. Suppose you determine midstream during the interview that the examples you have given are poor; you surrender to a loss. But, remember: it is not up to you to disqualify your candidacy—that is up to the interviewer, so do not do his job for him. Instead, concentrate on your job, which is to do the best you can in the interview. When you answer a question poorly, let go of your disappointment and start fresh with the next question. Interviewers recognize that a candidate's apprehension is part of the process and are willing to overlook one or two weakly worded answers.

Another way that a negative mind-set is revealed is if you take a defensive stance, especially in response to the interviewer's reactions to your examples. Follow-up questions are part of the competency-based interview, so expect to hear questions like, "What happened next?" or, "Can you explain your thought process?" The follow-up questions are a sincere attempt to clarify your experiences and uncover the depth of your knowledge.

It is also important to note that making false claims is never a good idea, but that during competency-based interviews, it is relatively easy for an interviewer to catch you in a white lie when follow-up questions are asked. If you exaggerate your level of experience, that quickly becomes evident. Remember, when you don't have actual examples to cite, answer the questions hypothetically, as described in Chapter 2.

A Potpourri of Other Interview Mistakes

Interviewers constantly encounter the classic interview missteps, which they have grown accustomed to expect. And with job competition so stiff, once a candidate makes a typical mistake, it is difficult to recover. Do not fall into any of these interview pitfalls:

1. *Taking Charge of the Interview.* Though it is true that a candidate is interviewing the company while the hiring manager is interviewing the candidate, some candidates are too aggressive about the former. They assume the role of interviewer and attempt to control the session. This power play never fares well for the candidate. Keep in mind that, just as you do not want to be interrogated, neither does the interviewer. As the job candidate, you should take an active role in the interview, but allow the interviewer to take the lead.

2. *Scheduling Interviews Too Close Together.* Competency-based interviews run long—sometimes sixty minutes or more. Schedule your interviews accordingly, so you don't put yourself in a situation of having to choose between cutting an interview short or arriving late to another.

3. *Believing the Interview Is a Gotcha Game.* One of the assets of competency-based interviews is that the interviewer lays the company's cards on the table. The questions that are asked reveal the proficiencies that are considered most important to the position. In addition, the questions reveal the problems you may encounter if hired. Keep those two things in mind when you start to feel that the questions are being asked just to trick you. When an interviewer asks competency-based questions, be assured that your answers are relevant to the position.

4. *Being Too Modest.* The main purpose of asking competency-based questions is to give you the opportunity to describe your assets. The in-

terviewer wants to learn about your successes, so this is not a time to be humble. Speak confidently about your relevant accomplishments, your experiences, and how you will add value to the hiring organization.

5. *Monitoring Your Time.* Though you may be anxious, avoid glancing at your watch. Competency-based interviews run long, and if you look at the time, the interviewer may conclude that you are not interested or are bored with the interview. To avoid giving the wrong impression, focus your attention solely on the interviewer.

Anyone can get tripped up during an interview by an unexpected question and can drift off course when giving a response. But when you are prepared with your list of core competencies and are aware of the common mistakes that can ruin the interview—the ones you can control—you're a long way toward eliminating the negatives. You are free to answer the competency-based questions to the best of your ability, without worrying about how you are coming across to the interviewer.

Seven Ways to Stand Out During the Interview

Interview preparation is essential. Laying the groundwork for a successful interview minimizes your anxiety and boosts your confidence, as well as your ability to think on your feet and provide the information interviewers need to make an educated hiring decision. Advanced preparation sets you up to deliver concise, competency-filled responses that address the requirements of the open position.

Advanced preparation will also allow you to stand out from the crowd—to differentiate yourself from all the other applicants, most of whom won't have done their homework. For instance, with a little preparation before the interview, you can determine your personal brand, find ways to control your anxiety, fine-tune your speaking voice to remove kinks or inflections that make you sound unprofessional, choose words in advance that will convey your message while also avoiding words that could sabotage your efforts, refine and reshape overly general statements, and script your answers so they are ready when you need them. This chapter helps you tackle these jobs and run toward the goal line.

Write a Personal Brand Statement

Whether you deliberately shaped your career with a personal brand in mind or not, you are recognized for your specific core competencies and personal characteristics. If your past is replete with proficiencies, you can easily draw a picture of yourself for each interview. If not, then you need to work up an image of yourself that constitutes a substantial brand—one that will be remembered after the interview.

Because your professional reputation hinges on your experience, it is important to follow two steps in creating your personal brand: (1) choose core competencies that describe your experience (revisit Chapter 1 to determine these); and (2) mention specific accomplishments that will pique the interest of a potential employer. Branding statements can also be used as the objective or profile for your résumé. For additional résumé objective samples, revisit Chapter 3.

Here are some examples of branding statements:

Sample 1: Marketing Professional. Comprehensive experience in directing and executing integrated marketing programs, including database modeling, direct mail, telemarketing initiatives, and Web site tracking. Established customer-driven objectives that included acquisition, value increase, and life-long retention.

Sample 2: Senior Consultant. Oversee engagements that involve multi-day, on-site interviews with key client team members from various departments, gathering data on policies/practices for record retention/management, regulatory compliance, and data review/production regarding legal data discovery requests. Contribute to the development of comprehensive recommendations to strengthen underperforming areas. Proven experience in negotiating services packages for deployment of e-mail archiving and electronic discovery solutions.

Sample 3: Sales Manager. Developed and implemented client acquisition, business development, and marketing strategies. Created partnership channels, secured corporate sponsorships, and participated in business development organizations to drive growth for start-up business.

Sample 4: Operations Management. Results-driven senior operating executive offering over fifteen years of experience and success in driving operational growth, leading start-up and turnaround efforts, maximizing business opportunities, and ensuring compliance w/ legal and regulatory requirements. Recognized agent for change with documented ability to lead reengineering activities that fulfilled strategic objectives. Hold JD and BA degrees.

Reduce Your Anxiety

Anxiety can place a chokehold on your interview performance. This affliction can be especially deadly during a competency-based interview, when you need to show clear understanding of the questions being asked and remain focused while you provide the answers to those questions. Apprehension usually creeps up when you lack the ability to adapt to the interview setting: you are being "tested," your knowledge or ability is being questioned, you are afraid of failing.

We are all individuals and we have different things that trigger our feelings of anxiety. It is up to you to recognize your own anxiety triggers and learn to minimize them before your heart begins to pound, you feel flushed, or you get tense and start to sweat.

To begin, remind yourself of the preparations you have made to be ready for the interview. There's another step you can take, once your appointment for the interview is set. Many times jobseekers are so excited to get an interview that they forget to ask who they are interviewing with. When you know the name of the interviewer, Google her name to find any information on the Internet regarding interview questions the person normally asks.

Then, you can control your anxiety to some extent by keeping the following thoughts in mind:

- ⊘ Realize that the interviewer wants you to succeed. She wants the search for a hiree to end just as much as you want a job offer.
- ⊘ Let go of the dream, and focus on the reality. Don't want the job so desperately before the interview that it clouds your perspective. In truth, you cannot know whether you want the position without discussing the specifics of the job with the hiring manager. For all you know, you may not be impressed by what the company has to offer.

⊘ A no result is not necessarily the worst thing that can happen to you because there is nothing worse than accepting a position that is not the right fit. You have probably been stuck in a job in which you did not get along with the manager or your values were not aligned with the corporation; that's a sticky situation and one that causes great stress. Receiving a no at the get-go may avoid that for you.

Improve Your Speaking Voice

Most of us are surprised to hear our own voice—and often we don't like how it sounds. Yet your speaking voice is important for a successful interview, that it not sound harsh or squeaky or even be just too loud or too soft. There's much about your voice you cannot change, but you certainly can make certain you project clarity and confidence at all times.

There are some easy steps you can take to improve the quality of your speaking voice. Beth Mann, of Hot Buttered Media, a full-service media and public relations firm, suggests the following techniques:

⊘ *Humming.* This is one of the easiest and most accessible ways to improve the quality of your voice. Rumor has it that Frank Sinatra used this technique as his only warm-up before singing onstage. To prove its efficacy, speak a sentence prior to humming, then hum for five minutes. Feel your lips vibrate. Hum high, hum low. Then speak the same sentence again. You will notice a cleaner, more forward sound. That is the natural sound and placement of your voice.

⊘ *Yawning.* Could this get any easier? That is right, yawn with sound (that natural "slide" sound from a high note to a low note). Do not feel like yawning? Then fake it. Try this a few times in a row. Notice the relaxed opening in the back of your throat. Most of us restrict this part of our throat, due to stress and fatigue. The idea is to keep the same open "yawn" sensation when we speak throughout the day.

⊘ *Donkey bray.* That is right, donkey bray. (You may want to do this one in private!) Bray like a donkey—let your lips flap together and include sound (similar to the yawn "slide"). Keep your lips loose and relaxed. Do this several times. Follow it up with some facial stretching—smile hard, then relax. Open your face as if to scream, hold for a second, then relax.

Finish up with some gentle head rolls. A relaxed face and neck are necessary vessels for a relaxed, assertive voice.

⊘ *T-time.* Enunciation is one of the weakest elements in most of our speech. Making some small changes in the way you pronounce words can change the way you are perceived. True or not, people who enunciate properly are often considered intelligent and well spoken. So how do you start cleaning up your speech? Say the words *notice* or *little.* If you "notice," you probably say something closer to "nodice" and "liddle," For one day, focus on your *T*s. You do not have to overdo it; small changes make a big difference.

⊘ *Let your words breathe.* Most of us have a tendency to speak in a "slurry" manner, sliding one word into another. Pretty soon, an entire sentence sounds like one word! Grab your nearest magazine or newspaper and read from it. Exaggerate each word, focusing on the separate quality of each and every word. While you may not want to speak like this on a daily basis, you will get a sense of what true enunciation is all about.

Be Concise

Words matter—not only the words you choose but also how you put them together. Since competency-based questions require detailed responses, wordiness—or convoluted and excessive language—can be a common result. You must find a balance between providing the detailed information required and speaking directly and simply become aware of common wordy expressions and avoid them. Figure 5-1 provides examples of wordy phrases and their concise equivalents.

Common Words and Phrases to Avoid

The words and phrases you select to communicate your experiences will impact the interviewer's perception of your qualifications. Certain common words may seem harmless to you, but they can be ammunition that shoots down the listener's perception of you. When the interviewer is offended by what you say or has a negative reaction to your use of slang, there's a breakdown in communication. To avoid this problem, familiar-

Figure 5-1

WORDINESS	CONCISE
on a daily basis	daily
on account of the fact that	because
in spite of	despite
a lot of	many
due to the fact that	because
later on	later
at that point in time	then
through the use of	through
in spite of the fact that	although
last but not least	finally
make contact with	contact
valuable asset	asset
in view of the fact that	because
later on	later
make a decision	decide
regardless of the fact	although
throughout the course of	throughout the
prior to	before
with the exception of	except for

ize yourself with the following conversational pitfalls that leave an unintentional negative impression.

1. *Do not refer to women as girls.* Though you may not mean harm, the interviewer may view you as sexist or as someone who may have problems working with women. Instead, refer to co-workers and others as team members or use particular job titles. For example, refer to "the receptionist," not as "the girl at the front desk." In a similar way, older candidates should avoid referring to younger co-workers as "kids." This implies a lack of respect for younger team members.

2. *Avoid slang.* Very casual talk does not have a place in an interview, and that includes bar talk, sports jargon, and all off-color references. Though many people use "you guys" when referring to co-workers in everyday situations, avoid the phrase.

3. *Drop "fillers" from your talk.* For example, eliminate any habitual use of *just* and *er* and *like,* as these indicate hesitancy and poor expressive ability. Likewise, using the phrases "I think" and "I guess" send a sub-liminal message that you lack confidence.

4. *Eliminate "qualifiers."* We often add small words that modify the meaning of the nouns that follow, but this is a bad habit because these words minimize the impact of those nouns. For example, do not use the word *try.* The statement, "I try my hardest to satisfy client expec-tations" is simply not as effective as, "I have a proven track record in client satisfaction."

Make Specific Statements

Because the purpose of competency-based questions is to solicit in-depth responses, you must steer clear of general statements. As an example, let's examine a common competency-based question asked of teachers: "Tell me about a time when you were proud to be an educator." Here are sev-eral ways to respond to this question:

> Version 1: "When I set up a school-wide talent show."
> Version 2: "When I set up a well-received school-wide talent show where students came together for an evening of rappers, gui-tarists, pianists, and singers."
> Version 3: "As a new music teacher for the Huntington School Dis-trict, I coordinated the school's first Music Talent Show Club. Along with club members, we planned the logistics for an evening show, which featured rappers, guitarists, pianists, and singers. Students, parents, teachers, and administrators were en-ergized, and that enthusiasm was felt throughout the school for several weeks."

Let's consider each alternative. Version 1 is bland and stops short of providing the interviewer with a well-rounded picture of the event. Though the interviewer may deduce the reason the talent show is an accomplishment the teacher is proud of, it is up to that teacher to offer an explanation.

Version 2 is an improvement. The answer provides the listener with detail; on the other hand, it does not give the interviewer all the information required to fully appreciate the extent of the teacher's experience. In both versions, the interviewer will most likely have to ask follow-up questions to solicit more information. And those follow-up questions break the momentum of the discussion. Lastly, version 3 offers all the interviewer needs to know: the situation, the action, and the result (SOAR; see Chapter 2). A well-thought-out response leaves the interviewer with a positive impression of experience.

Script or Outline Your Responses

There is no right or wrong method to prepare your answers for interview questions. It is a matter of preference and comfort. You can choose to script your responses whereby you flesh out your thoughts, or you can create an outline with answers for the questions that may be asked.

There is a sense of security to be gained in writing down, word-for-word, your answers to potential interview questions. This method will make you brainstorm your answers and to think through your work experiences. There's a caveat, however: becoming too accustomed to delivering perfect answers may cause you to freeze during the actual interview and you may "go blank" when off-the-cuff answers are required. Also, following a script too closely may make you sound stiff. On the other hand, scripting your responses keeps your professional history and accomplishments at the forefront of your thinking. You will find scripted responses in Chapters 6 through 10.

In contrast, outlining your responses—say, on index cards, on which you write a question and a short list of answers—may allow you more flexibility during the interview. With ready answers, during the interview you won't trip over your words trying to remember every detail. Also, you will sound more natural. See Figure 5-2 for an example of an index card prepared as an outline response.

In short, anything that you can do to make yourself stand out from the other candidates is a step in the right direction. By following the suggestions in this chapter, you will approach the competency-based interview confident and prepared.

Figure 5-2

Sample Interview Question

Describe a time a customer was not happy with company policies and procedures.

SITUATION: Oversaw day-to-day operations for retail location

ACTION: Arranged merchandise displays

RESULT: Effectively maximized sales by twenty percent

Part II

Competency-Based Questions and Answers

Chapter 6

Competency #1 — Individual Responsibility

Along with evaluating your accomplishments and how you work in a team environment (see Chapter 10 for team-oriented competency-based questions), interviewers will view your individual characteristics—those traits that demonstrate who you are, what your ambitions are, and how you manage work situations on your own. Specifically, interviewers will closely inspect the following core competencies that pertain to individual responsibility: decisiveness, independence, flexibility, and career goals.

Decisiveness

Taking a decisive approach when managing organizational issues demonstrates your assurance in your ability to make the right decisions. Interviewers will evaluate your self-confidence and observe how that translates to your work life.

Key Behaviors and Career Values

A. **Thoughtful.** Attentive to surroundings, circumstances, and the people at work (i.e., colleagues, business associates, vendors, and clients) in order to make conscientious decisions.

Example: _____

_____

_____

B. **Deductive Reasoning.** Takes into consideration every aspect of a problem and reflects on the impact and implications of each option.

Example: _____

_____

_____

C. **Results Driven.** Produces effective, timely results through the execution of strategic or tactical planning.

Example: _____

_____

_____

D. **Analytical.** Ability to examine and base important decisions using limited resources.

Example: _____

_____

_____

E. **Goal Oriented.** Establishes objectives, monitors progress, and measures attainment of goals.

Example: _____

_____

_____

F. **Strategic Thinking.** Makes decisions that have immediate and long-term effects on the organization's bottom line and/or productivity.

Example: _____

_____

_____

G. **Shift Perspective.** Ability to understand opposing arguments and formulate a plan based on more than one viewpoint.

Example: _____

_____

_____

H. **Logical Sense.** Makes sound and well-informed decisions to implement business plans.

Example: _____

_____

_____

I.   **Strong Intuition.** Incorporates gut instincts into thinking that comes up with the best possible solutions.

Example: _____

_____

_____

J. **Problem Solving.** Defines the parameters of a problem and extracts pertinent information to develop a solution with little room for error.

Example: _____

_____

_____

Interview Questions and Answers

Question 1. There are times when a firm decision must be made quickly, and there are other times when it is prudent to consider all angles before reaching a conclusion. Give an example of a situation when you took time in making a final decision.

SITUATION: One of the first assignments I tackled at Trucking Services, Inc., was to monitor the delay of international shipments. For an unknown reason, packages were not arriving at distributors on time.

ACTION: As the first course of action, I joined the production line to get a hands-on feel for the shipping process. This step allowed me to pinpoint the lag in production time and determine the next course of action.

RESULT: I recommended logistic solutions that took into consideration the different configurations of the packages, including varying weights and dimensions. Once the new system was in place, the orders arrived as scheduled.

Question 2. Rarely do issues arise that are one-dimensional. With that fact in mind, describe a time you handled a situation that had different layers.

SITUATION: At Management Properties, I was charged with spear-heading a four-phase, seven-hundred-unit redevelopment, which included two condos, multiple townhouses, and a ninety-one multi-office facility. There were many initiatives I had to manage in order to receive approval for all the construction efforts.

ACTION: To ensure that everything went off without a hitch, I diligently cut through a lot of red tape, including completing necessary paperwork, obtaining necessary licenses, and attending town meetings. In addition, I networked with local business and community leaders to receive their buy-in on the project's large scope.

RESULT: Based on my efforts, I delivered positive results, including a town vote by unanimous approval to green-light the construction. Conse-quently, each phase of the project was completed within the specified time schedule and within budget requirements.

Question 3. Tell me about a time when you encountered competing deadlines and you had to choose one deadline to fall by the wayside in order to meet the others.

SITUATION: Though there are occasions when I am pulled in multiple directions, there has never been a time when I dropped the ball. That said, I will gladly share a situation when I managed to juggle my time. In one partic-ular instance, I was on my way to meet a client at a press conference when I received a desperate call on my cell from another client, asking for assis-tance in managing a crisis that just unfolded.

ACTION: Since I could not be in two places at the same time, I requested the assistance of another senior-level staff member, who gladly agreed to lend a hand.

RESULT: We split the responsibilities. I attended the press conference, and once it was over, I rushed back to the office to co-manage my other client's crisis.

Question 4. It is impossible to please every staff member or client. Describe a time when you made an unpopular decision.

Situation: As a result of a sluggish economy, Mohalden Track's bottom line had suffered a great deal. As the CFO, my recommendation was to cut staff. It was the first time in the company's history when we had to consider layoffs. I knew the board needed solid evidence before approving such a measure.

Action: From my experience with the board, I knew that their decision to green-light the layoffs would hinge on the treatment of outgoing employees. As part of the proposal, I included a cost-benefit analysis of the downsizing effort; and I incorporated a generous severance package for the soon-to-be-displaced employees.

Result: The board members listened intently, asked a lot of questions, and ultimately voted for the layoff cycle I suggested. The cuts revitalized company profits and 25 percent of the laid-off employees were rehired within the year.

Question 5. Recall a time when you were approached to take sides on an issue, but decided to stay neutral.

Situation: There was a time when a supervisor complained about an employee's performance. After objectively reviewing her report, I came to the conclusion that most of the concerns were minor and that there was only one serious offense.

Action: I advised the supervisor to let go of some of the points she may have found annoying but that did not break company policy. During our discussion, I emphasized how important it was for managers to focus on bigger issues and not get bogged down with details. In addition, I agreed to talk to the employee about her overall behavior, making sure I touched on the fact that the supervisor is entitled to manage the department to ensure productivity.

Result: The performance concerns that required attention were resolved, without incident. For the remaining years that the employee was on staff, she was never again called into my office for a job-related problem.

Question 6. Tell me about a time when you came up with a way to increase output.

SITUATION: At Medical Facility Associates, the percentage of invoices paid by carriers had decreased at an alarming rate.

ACTION: As a course of action was to determine the root cause of this decrease. After a review of the records, it was evident that the billing coordinators needed training on handling the carrier's new policies. I called an emergency meeting that focused on two priorities: educating the staff on the health carrier's new codes and showing them how they could navigate the maze required to receive payment for patient procedures.

RESULT: After the training, the billing coordinators resubmitted the invoices following the proper procedures, and the facility received payment with no further hiccups.

Question 7. Describe an occasion when you made a decision that could have had a negative impact on the company if not managed correctly.

OBSTACLE: Blue Cosmetics' global popularity was at an all-time high. Domestic sales were through the roof, but internationally we were losing money, owing to badly negotiated business contracts overseas.

ACTION: Since we could not continue to conduct business worldwide at a loss, I revisited the foreign currency agreements with our distributors, keeping in mind the current rate of inflation. This was a tricky proposition, because I had to convince the partners to accept new contract terms at a time when the existing agreements were still in effect. I leveraged my personal relationships to get each of the distributors, individually, to consent to the changes.

RESULT: The renegotiations ran smoothly, and I was able to secure competitive contracts with our international business partners that met Blue Cosmetics' net and gross profit margins.

Question 8. Give an example of a time when you were surprised by an unexpected situation and had to change course quickly.

SITUATION: In order to increase profits at the clinic, management wanted to expand our clinical services to include residents with schizophrenia. No one on staff had experience treating schizophrenic patients. Staff members approached me to represent the team and bring our concerns to management.

ACTION: I summarized our concerns, and I provided a list of initiatives we could implement to prepare the department for the new population. Our immediate supervisor agreed to discuss the suggestions with upper management.

RESULT: To the team's surprise, he never met with the executives. When the patients arrived, we all pulled together to provide the best service possible, with the resources available to us.

Question 9. Recall a time when you used good judgment and logic in solving a problem.

SITUATION: Jupe, Inc.'s quest to go green was an opportunity to implement an idea that would save the company money and, at the same time, was environmentally sound.

ACTION: I met with members of Marketing and Advertising to discuss the possibility of using recyclable materials and of reducing the package size for our perfume line.

RESULT: Smaller packaging and recyclable materials cost less to manufacture. In addition, more packages fit into the trucks and that translated to greater distribution with fewer trips, so fuel costs were reduced as well.

Question 10. Tell me about a time when you thought a problem was resolved, only to find out that you were mistaken.

SITUATION: As an associate for General Insurance Agency, I misquoted a homeowner's policy and I called the customer to let her know. During our conversation, she accepted my apology and agreed to sign on at the proper quote. I thought the matter was closed. Then a month later, the agency received a letter from the insurance carrier stating that the customer had filed a complaint because she thought I was price-gouging, owing to the coastal location.

ACTION: I drafted a letter to the carrier, explaining that the error occurred because the property appraiser's paperwork was incorrect. The application stated that she lived in Palm Beach County, when in fact her residence was in West Palm Beach County. I took full responsibility, saying that instead of double-checking the paperwork, I simply provided a quote.

RESULT: Needless to say, from that moment forward I double-checked the information provided in every appraiser's report, and I never encountered another situation where I misquoted a policy.

Question 11. Not all problems have clear-cut solutions. Give an example of a difficult decision you made and your thought process for making it.

SITUATION: The Odd Place was going through a tough financial crisis. We cut back on miscellaneous needs, such as office supplies, cellphone usage, and lunches. However, those reductions were not enough.

ACTION: After reviewing options, including laying off employees, I determined that the best choice was to pass a twelve percent increase in cost of medical insurance on to the associates.

RESULT: That was a decision I made with a heavy heart, but it was better than any alternative. Though employees preferred not to pay additional fees for their health-care plan, they understood the situation and were thankful to have a job when so many of their neighbors did not.

Question 12. Summarize a time when you managed a situation characterized by high pressure.

OBSTACLE: When I worked for Wingate Hotels, I returned from vacation to find that the benefits coordinator had given notice the day I left for my vacation. Ultimately, that left me one week to aggressively recruit candidates, catch up with outstanding problems, and document position procedures.

ACTION: To expedite matters, I wrote a classified ad, posted it online, and also called a recruitment agency for their assistance.

RESULT: I took on the administrative functions of the area until a new coordinator was hired and trained.

Independence

Making smart, independent decisions that lead to your department's successes is important information that an interviewer will try to uncover during an interview.

Key Behaviors and Career Values

A. **Autonomous.** Ability to work with limited supervision.

Example: _____

_____

_____

B. **Proactive and Assertive.** Motivated to complete projects on time and within budget.

Example: _____

_____

_____

C. **Dependable.** Recognized by management and peers as a reliable person who can be counted on to meet prescribed obligations.

Example: _____

_____

_____

D. **Self-Confident.** Poised individual who conveys confidence when communicating with others and meeting responsibilities.

Example: _____

_____

_____

E. **Self-Reliant.** Relies on personal experiences, judgments, and past resources to come up with solutions and execute projects.

Example: _____

_____

_____

F. **Accountable.** Directs actions and takes responsibility for both positive and negative results.

Example: _____

_____

_____

G. **Risk Taker.** Takes chances and goes the extra mile to seize opportunities.

Example: _____

_____

_____

H. **Persistent.** Determined to finish assignments or projects in a timely manner.

Example: _____

_____

_____

I. **Resourceful.** Uses research materials efficiently and puts knowledge to good use.

Example: _____

_____

_____

J. **Critical Thinker.** Anticipates the next steps in a process and develops tactics to overcome obstacles before they arise.

Example: _____

_____

_____

Interview Questions and Answers

Question 13. Because not everyone always agrees with every company policy, tell me about a time when you spoke up against a standard procedure.

SITUATION: When employed by Family and Children Service Incorporated, I conducted individual therapy sessions and provided case management for clients with chronic mental illness. Compared with the psychiatrists who met with clients only every three months, as the therapist I met with these clients once a week. This allowed me to build rapport with the patients, and I was able to leverage those relationships during interdisciplinary meetings with the psychiatrists. I found that many times patients failed to provide their psychiatrists with the proper history of their medication intake.

ACTION: As a result, it was up to me to advocate for appropriate dosages when the psychiatrists were set to prescribe the wrong amount.

RESULT: Since I kept careful documentation of patient meetings, the psychiatrists highly regarded my input and made adjustments with my recommendations in mind.

Question 14. This division is a department of one. The person hired will be required to manage problems on his or her own. Please describe a time when you dealt with a situation without receiving input from staff members.

SITUATION: At MRI Technology, I am surrounded by technicians and doctors who do not have information technology (IT) experience. Since I am the only IT professional on staff, whenever a computer issue arises, I have to solve it myself—there is no one else I can turn to for assistance.

ACTION: With no supervision, it is up to me to identify the problems and find the solutions. Using my knowledge of computers, I figure out the solution most of the time. For those that are beyond my reach, I rely on a network of professionals with whom I have built relationships over the years.

RESULT: As a result, I have gained a reputation from management and peers for being a resourceful individual who is never stumped by a computer problem.

Question 15. Working in a team environment has its benefits. Likewise, working independently is also rewarding. Provide an example of a time when you were commended for your ability to complete a task on your own.

SITUATION: When you are working on an assembly line, it is important to inspect every part thoroughly before releasing it to the next stage of production.

ACTION: I take great care in self-auditing the parts, ensuring that each meets the quality standards set by the company.

RESULT: When the quality assurance representative comes by my station, I always receive a 100 percent grade on the inspection—a rating I share with only one other team member.

Question 16. Describe an occasion when you managed a situation that was your supervisor's responsibility.

OBSTACLE: While working at Amore International and Company, my supervisor was set to go on maternity leave. Before her departure, we went over the tasks that I was to manage in her absence.

ACTION: During one of our meetings, I broached the subject of rewriting job descriptions while she was away. This was a project she had on her to-do list for quite some time but had never gotten around to starting. Without hesitation she agreed. Together we drew up a plan of action that I was to follow.

RESULT: When she came back from her leave, she reviewed the rewritten job descriptions and approved each after making only minor changes. Soon thereafter, the employees were provided with the new descriptions and, in most cases, a raise as well.

Question 17. Describe a time when you felt constraints placed on you that worked against completing your job effectively.

SITUATION: Over the last few years, the public school system has changed from a student-centered curriculum to being state-based. Instead of teaching phonics and grammar, my main responsibility is to prepare the class for mandatory tests. Such requirements do not allow room for originality in the classroom.

ACTION: For an opportunity to put my teaching skills to full use, I applied to The Science Forum Charter School.

RESULT: There, I have the opportunity to engage students in learning, in a way that I was not able to in the past. Successfully, I instilled a love for science in the students that will carry them through to adulthood.

Question 18. Give an example of a situation in which you were selected over your peers to complete a project.

SITUATION: At Mallory Paints, we had several divisions that competed in the marketplace. For example, one division marketed premium paint and another had second-rate paint. Instead of the brand managers' structuring their prices to rival outside competition, they competed with each other.

ACTION: As part of a special project, I was chosen to conduct external competitive intelligence. I took special care in analyzing the competitors' products and used the information to also evaluate internal price points.

RESULT: Within a year, I restructured the pricing strategy to reflect two price increases that competed with the opposition and not with the company's internal products. The efforts achieved a boost of $3 million in unexpected operating income.

Question 19. Tell me about a time when you lacked experience in a specific area and needed to outsource an initiative.

SITUATION: When I was the operations manager for Clothing Retail, I wanted to apply segmentation strategies to determine customer buying preferences. With such a tool we could analyze customer age, gender, interests, and spending habits, subsequently raising profits.

ACTION: Since this was an information technology initiative beyond my know-how, I outsourced the project to a software company that specialized in developing frequent-buyer programs.

RESULT: Based on the information we gathered, we could offer loyal customers specials and discounts. This preferential treatment was appreciated by the consumers and foot traffic increased during the holiday season.

Question 20. Describe an occasion when you were left to your own devices to manage a situation.

SITUATION: As the night maintenance guy for Zenith Hotels, I serve as a jack-of-all-trades, from preparing conference rooms for early-morning meetings to making small repairs to the plumbing and electricity, it is my job to know it all.

ACTION: One night there was a broken pipe that gushed water onto the main floor of the hotel. From reading the electronic monitoring system, I pinpointed the area and was able to contain the situation until a certified plumber could arrive in the morning.

RESULT: My ability to manage the situation on my own saved the hotel what could have been high costs for repairing extensive damage.

Question 21. Tell me about a time when your success was dependent on another's decision.

OBSTACLE: At the Women's Correctional Center, I was hired to maintain the integrity of the adult basic education program within the prison system.

ACTION: Part of my responsibility was to write monthly and quarterly status reports for the Department of Education. In these reports, I noted program changes and provided statistical information on the participants, including TABE pretest and posttest and GED scores.

RESULT: The information I provided was analyzed by a government entity. Since future program funding was based on these findings, I made sure my data were meticulously accurate and included all the information required, so the program would be properly subsidized.

Question 22. Describe a time when you went against the status quo.

OBSTACLE: After an internal audit of the Maximum Wellness employee files, it came to our attention that a long-time clerical staff member, who was privy to confidential files, had falsified information on her employment application.

ACTION: Under other circumstances, I might have fired her on the spot. But she was well liked by everyone in the office, and her performance evaluations highlighted her commitment to the organization. After two weeks of gathering information from Legal, I made the decision not to terminate her employment. Instead, I transferred her to a parallel position where she did not have access to private files.

RESULT: As I suspected, the employee continued to do a stellar job and she stayed with the company until her retirement.

Question 23. Tell me about a time where you managed a situation on your own while simultaneously adjusting to changes that you had no control over.

SITUATION: When I worked at Job Lot, a long-term associate suddenly passed away. It was a personal and professional blow to everyone in the division. After careful consideration, management decided not to restaff the position, and instead chose to split the workload between a co-worker and me.

ACTION: With much of the work I had just inherited coming with deadlines, I prioritized my existing responsibilities to accommodate the new ones.

RESULT: By coming in early and working through my lunch hour, I successfully met all the deadlines.

Question 24. Recall a time when you made an independent decision.

OBSTACLE: When I worked as an administrator for Delish Culinary School, the instructors would submit a list of ingredients they needed in order to teach each day's lesson. Every day at noon, the deliveries arrived, and we were pressed for time to stock each instruction room before the afternoon classes began.

ACTION: I rescheduled the deliveries for earlier in the day so that we had enough time to organize the rooms.

RESULT: The workday flow was better organized, and if ingredients were missing, we had time to get them before classes started.

Flexibility

The work environment requires flexibility—from dealing with differing employee and customer personality styles to tackling an unexpected project that hit your desk five minutes before closing time. Interviewers will focus some of their questions on your ability to adapt to various situations.

Key Behaviors and Career Values

A. **Versatile.** Open and ready to accept changes in policies and procedures.

Example: _____

_____

_____

B. **Adaptable.** Adjusts rapidly to changes in the work environment.

Example: _____

_____

_____

C. **Go-Getter Attitude.** Promotes the advancement of the department by volunteering for assignments.

Example: _____

_____

_____

D. **Easygoing.** Easily switches gears from one function to another, without getting overwhelmed.

Example: _____

_____

_____

E. **Responsive.** Reacts appropriately when escalating situations arise.

Example: _____

_____

_____

F. **Receptive.** Implements an open-minded approach and a willingness to listen to new ideas.

Example: _____

_____

_____

G. **Approachable.** Friendly and easy to talk to in a variety of situations, especially those that are stressful and demanding.

Example: _____

_____

_____

H. **Multi-Tasker.** Performs varying tasks at once, while staying calm and collected.

Example: _____

_____

_____

I.   **Accepts Criticism.** Values constructive feedback and takes such as an opportunity to grow professionally.

Example: _____

_____

_____

J. **Accommodating.** Takes into account the particular situations and personalities when managing projects or people.

Example: _____

_____

_____

Interview Questions and Answers

Question 25. Tell me about a time when you had to adjust to a different work environment.

SITUATION: When I reentered the teaching field, after serving as a guidance counselor for six years, I had to readjust to the classroom environment.

ACTION: In preparation, I went to a teacher's conference, where the speakers discussed topics such as behavior modification techniques as a motivator, manipulative implementation, and instituting a Balanced Literacy Program.

RESULT: After the conference I was better prepared to manage students and meet district expectations. As a result, I successfully engaged students in the learning process.

Question 26. Describe an occasion when there was a fundamental change in the way things were done in your workplace. What was your response to it?

SITUATION: When Bank of the States merged with Capital Financial Firm, we expected a smooth transition because both companies provided the same products and services. However, I was surprised to learn that my role as a customer service representative changed from that of simply attending to customer inquiries to also including sales of bank products and services.

ACTION: Unlike my peers, I did not quit or complain to management. I understood that there is more than one way to accomplish your goals. To ensure that I had a grasp of my new responsibilities, I asked questions during the training sessions.

RESULT: Within three months, there were layoffs but my position remained intact. My manager told me that I was not affected by the reorganization because of my commitment to embracing the bank's new procedures.

Question 27. Recall the last time you felt energized about a project.

SITUATION: When my employer, Interior Specialty Group, merged with The Summit Company, I was excited about the partnership. Both companies were boutique firms with solid reputations in the industry. I recognized that the alliance would attract larger, more challenging deals from influential clients. As I suspected, within weeks we landed a contract with a Fortune 500 company to launch a big marketing campaign.

ACTION: As part of a team, I helped market the company's software products to various media, including newspapers, TV, magazines, and Web sites.

RESULT: The campaign was a success, and I was assigned to additional high-profile accounts.

Question 28. Give an example of a situation in which you assessed a person's temperament and how that assessment helped the relationship.

SITUATION: An employee was extremely sensitive, and team members felt they could not express themselves without that employee's taking offense. For example, if a co-worker walked into the office but did not greet her, she felt like the co-worker did not like or was upset with her.

ACTION: I realized that this employee was overly sensitive, and so I had to flex my communication style so she wouldn't feel under attack. I decided to have a casual conversation with her instead of setting up a meeting. This approach disarmed her, and I was able to broach the subject without her trepidation. During our talk, I encouraged her to not personalize the behaviors of others. I also explained that people have lives outside of the office that can impact their moods—for instance, some people are not "morning people"—and she should accept that others' statements are not necessarily directed toward her.

RESULT: Since no one's personality or outlook changes overnight, I had to meet with her a few more times to help her work through her emotions and focus her energy on work projects instead. That said, over time she grasped the notion that, in a work environment, a thick skin is sometimes required.

Question 29. Tell me about a time when you had to adjust your priorities to meet someone else's higher priority.

SITUATION: Every day I create a to-do list that helps me prioritize the day's activities. One particular day I was going to make follow-up calls to generate new clients. Right after the day started, I received a call from a client who said that their system was down. A technician was on his way to fix the problem, but since I was the one who sold her the equipment a week earlier, she wanted me on-site as well.

ACTION: To maintain goodwill, I put aside my to-do list and served as the liaison between the client and the technician.

RESULT: Later on that day, I received a call from the client's manager. He personally thanked me for taking the time to ensure that the system was up and running. When the company was ready to upgrade, I received the call to make that sale.

Question 30. Describe the culture of your organization and provide an example of how you work within this culture to achieve a goal.

SITUATION: In the organizational culture of the company I work for, employees are often required to work after normal hours. For example, as the organization partners with community businesses and participates in outreach events, I am required to attend those events in the evenings and on weekends.

ACTION: To strike a balance between my personal and professional life, I negotiated flex time whereby I could take late and extended lunches so I could attend my daughter's soccer games.

RESULT: The arrangement worked well because I was able to support my daughter and also meet the demands of the department and community-involvement initiatives.

Question 31. Give an example of a time when your patience was tested. How did you handle it?

Obstacle: When I worked for the Citizenship Enterprise, the media department had an affinity for meetings. We had two meetings per week, and most were unproductive because the head manager resisted planning in advance. His thought was that unstructured meetings led to greater creativity, and although his philosophy had merit, unfortunately in practice this hardly ever worked in his favor.

ACTION: In an effort to increase productivity, I started to e-mail him the talking points I wanted to broach during the meeting, and I asked for his input on these. After a few weeks, he began to request that all team members e-mail him their agendas for the meetings.

RESULT: As a result, the meetings were structured, and we were able to get more done in less time; regular meetings were reduced to two per month, as well.

Question 32. Describe a time when you were on the verge of completing a task and were asked to abandon the project for another project.

SITUATION: This is a common occurrence in the conference-catering business. There are a lot of activities to manage, from preparing standardized recipes to communicating with the general manager. One particular time, the kitchen equipment at Nickel and Wood Country Club failed one hour before guests were set to arrive. I was in the meeting hall supervising the layout of the room when I received notice of the breakdown.

ACTION: Since I could not be in two places at the same time, I walked my assistant through the arrangement requirements and asked her to monitor the execution of the plans while I went to find a technician to come fix the equipment on short notice.

RESULT: I made several phone calls and requested a favor to get a qualified technician onsite, who agreed to keep the cost down while completing the work quickly. By the time the guests arrived, everything was in place and no one had a clue of the mishap that had occurred right before their arrival.

Question 33. Give an example of a situation in which you worked for a company where your flexibility skills were important.

SITUATION: As a management trainee for Zenith Enterprise, I was required to learn every aspect of the company, from customer service to business administration initiatives.

ACTION: Regardless of the position I was in, I took the responsibilities seriously. I learned the inner workings of the different departments and the varying personalities who made up a division.

RESULT: Now, when I work in a specific department, I am mindful of the needs of cooperating departments and their deadlines. This perspective allows me to work collaboratively with other departments to meet overall objectives.

Question 34. Describe a time when you were required to go to work unexpectedly.

OBSTACLE: The day I was set to leave town for my sister's wedding, I received a call from *The Daily Press* editor, who asked me to interview the police and write a story about a string of robberies in the area. Though working late hours, getting phone calls in the middle of the night, and attending to last-minute edit requests are the norm for a freelance reporter, this time I was in a tight spot.

ACTION: Since I did not want to disappoint the editor, I postponed my departure until the next morning.

RESULT: I am known to work best under pressure, so when I delivered the story before the deadline, the editor was not surprised and was pleased that the article did not need revision.

Question 35. Tell me about a time when you altered your work pattern in order to complete a task.

SITUATION: During a stable economy, clients keep tabs on their portfolios from a distance. As the economy grows sluggish, those clients expect personal contact at least twice a week.

ACTION: To accommodate the clients' needs and keep my base satisfied, I contacted everyone on my list, regardless of whether I had news to share.

RESULT: I received kudos from clients, who commended me for keeping in touch during difficult times. Knowing that I was working diligently on their portfolios calmed some of their fears, especially when their friends said that their financial advisors had gone into hiding during tough times.

Question 36. Recall a situation in which you had to please more than one person at the same time.

SITUATION: As an administrative assistant for Malloy and Associates, I support three executives, each of whom has his own needs and requirements. Many times I am charged with managing different projects at the same time, as well. However, this is not as difficult as it sounds. The tasks always fall into the same categories, so I am able to complete each without changing gears.

ACTION: For example, when one executive hands me a copying task, I inform the other two that I am heading to the copy room. This is their opportunity to also hand me materials that need duplicating.

RESULT: Combining my tasks eliminates the need for additional trips to the copy room and opens up my day to manage other responsibilities.

Question 37. Describe an occasion when you dealt with an employee whose demeanor was causing a problem.

OBSTACLE: An employee at Dunst and Robertson constantly became defensive when asked the status of his projects. He blamed others for delays and never accepted responsibility when his projects were behind schedule.

ACTION: I had several meetings with him that focused on the importance of personal accountability. To complement our discussions, I encouraged him to enroll in a training course that centered on workflow prioritization.

RESULT: He successfully completed the course. In addition, his complaints lessened over time and his projects were completed in a timely manner.

Question 38. Describe a time when your work complemented another staff member's objective.

SITUATION: As an art teacher with Brownstone Elementary, I attend meetings with classroom teachers. During these get-togethers, we discussed the principal lessons that were scheduled and I found ways to adjust the art curriculum to reinforce the main lessons.

ACTION: For example, students were learning geography and studying the seven continents in their classrooms. To support their learning, I had the students make African-inspired jewelry in art class.

RESULT: Integrating art projects with regular classroom instruction offered the students an opportunity to see their education in more than one capacity, and helping them retain information at the same time.

Question 39. Give an example of a time when you offered your resignation.

SITUATION: I worked for a company that serviced credit card accounts, and I was responsible for persuading retailers to switch over to Merchant Express. I excelled in the position, attaining the best closure rate of all new hires. Unfortunately, after a month, I started to receive phone calls from my clients because they were dissatisfied with the service.

ACTION: I immediately called my supervisor to go over the list of complaints and find ways to rectify client concerns. During the meeting, I was informed that my job was to sell the product, not to return customer phone calls after the sales were made. Despite my apprehension about ignoring these customers, I was told I had no choice, since that was company procedure.

RESULT: Within twenty-four hours of that conversation, I gave my resignation. The company's protocol was not one I was comfortable with, and I found another position where customer needs were appreciated.

Career Goals

Your career goals and how they fit with the interviewing company's mission are important points that interest interviewers.

Key Behaviors and Career Values

A. **Future-focused.** Strengthens career aspects by anticipating change, taking his or her career seriously, and making a conscious effort to move that career forward.

Example: _____

_____

_____

B. **Recognizes personal weaknesses.** Identifies areas that need improvement and develops a plan to overcome them.

Example: _____

_____

_____

C. **Pursues self-development.** Takes an active interest in gaining knowledge in a variety of areas, including computer skills, leadership, and relationship building.

Example: _____

_____

_____

D. **Steadfast learner.** Implements lessons from past experiences to succeed in future endeavors.

Example: _____

_____

_____

E. **Sets performance goals.** Establishes sharp and clearly defined objectives geared to career advancement.

Example: _____

_____

_____

F. **Progressive mind-set.** Throughout the years, has received either promotions or increases in responsibilities.

Example: _____

_____

_____

G. **Sets priorities.** Makes direct efforts in specific areas so as to not get overwhelmed by competing objectives.

Example: _____

_____

_____

H. **Takes on new challenges.** Creates new opportunities to stimulate professional growth.

Example: _____

_____

_____

I. **Shows tenacity**. Displays a strong resolve to meet self-prescribed expectations.

Example: _____

_____

_____

J. **Makes careful decisions**. Applies reason to reach decisions that open doors to opportunities.

Example: _____

_____

_____

Interview Questions and Answers

Question 40. Recall a time when you made a difficult career move.

SITUATION: When Time Media Corporation merged with Media Elite, I was offered a promotion. Unfortunately, the acquisition meant that the organization became a publicly owned company. As such, I recognized that, with the union of both companies, the corporate culture would change from being customer-centric to investor-centric. Though I understood the value of a public company, my preference is to work for a privately held organization where there is more freedom to take business aspirations to the next level while simultaneously enhancing the client experience.

ACTION: As a result, I resigned from the company. That said, to ensure that I assisted in the transition period, I agreed to stay on until a replacement was found.

RESULT: After three months of recruitment and training efforts, a qualified candidate took over my responsibilities. And soon after that, I accepted a position with another organization where I was a better fit.

Question 41. Describe a time when a company you worked for invested in you professionally.

SITUATION: When I worked for Steel Mandates, company policy stated that after a year of employment, employees could pursue their master's degree on the owner's dime.

ACTION: I took advantage of the program. In fact, I was only one of two in the company's history to take advantage of the generous policy.

RESULT: Though there was no requirement that I stay working for Steel once I graduated, I have a strong sense of loyalty and I stayed with the company to assist in its market growth. I remained employed by the company until the owner passed away, and the business was sold.

Question 42. Tell me about a time when you accepted a position that you regretted.

SITUATION: Straight out of college, I was offered two positions—one as a case manager for a group home that serviced teenagers, and the other as a patient advocate for a hospital. Owing to student loans, I took the patient advocate position because the pay was $5,000 more a year. However, within a month of employment, I realized that I preferred to work with teenagers than with patients in a hospital.

ACTION: Since I made a commitment to the hospital, I stayed for a year, and I managed my caseload with care. I received many letters from patients and their families that highlighted the compassion and kindness I demonstrated on a daily basis.

RESULT: Once the year was up, I searched for a position I could be passionate about and gave my two weeks' notice. I have focused my career on working with adolescents ever since.

Question 43. Give an example of a situation in which you took specific steps to meet your career goals.

SITUATION: Right after high school, I went to work for a retail store. There I moved up the ladder as far as I could without a college degree.

ACTION: At the age of thirty-nine, while still employed full time at the store, I enrolled in a four-year business administration program at a local college.

RESULT: Upon graduating, and based on my work experience, the retail store offered me a position in the accounting department, where I was charged with account-receivable functions.

Question 44. Describe a time when you asked management for direct feedback.

SITUATION: When I was a junior staff member for Scottish Patches, I petitioned to join the team slated to deliver a high-impact presentation to a

Fortune Ten company. I wrote a proposal outlining the reasons I would be an asset to the team. The head of the department was impressed by my initiative, and agreed to let me serve on the team.

ACTION: I took great care in researching and putting together my part of the presentation. Since this was the first of its kind that I had participated in, I ran a few notes by the team leader for his constructive feedback.

RESULT: He added his thoughts on how to make the presentation even stronger, but overall, I was on the right track.

Question 45. Sometimes people have to take up opportunities to achieve professional success. Tell me about a time when you took a chance in your career and the result.

SITUATION: Throughout my career I worked for stable companies. However, when an opportunity to work with a construction startup presented itself, I was drawn in by the calculated risk involved. In addition, the role as construction manager intrigued me, since it meant greater responsibility as well.

ACTION: As part of the startup initiative, I established a market presence, developed OSHA guidelines, and created the budget workflow.

RESULT: Single-handedly I accelerated territory growth and cultivated a customer database, growing annual sales from zero to $11 million in a year.

Question 46. Describe an occasion when you expanded your knowledge base to further your career.

SITUATION: I enjoy technical writing, but it is formulaic. With the growing popularity of blogs, I wanted to take a crack at writing a TV show review site. After reviewing several well-known blogs in the same general area, I found a niche that could balance professionalism with a snarky approach.

ACTION: Since that type of writing was new to me, I contacted several blog sites and agreed to write for a nonpaying Web site about the first season of *The Comedy Hour.* I figured that the experience and exposure would pave the way to a paying job.

RESULT: Once I developed an online portfolio, I used it to apply for top reviewer sites. For the past three years, I have been writing part time for *Rate This,* one of the most popular online review sites.

Question 47. Tell me about a time when you leveraged your past experience to advance your career.

SITUATION: After years of teaching biology to ninth-grade students, I wanted to change gears and be a teacher consultant, a position in which I would train high school educators on how to include the ideas in current science textbooks in their lesson plans.

ACTION: I contacted a friend who was a textbook sales representative and asked whether he could serve as a reference, using his affiliation with his employer, Advanced Books. Because of our longstanding friendship, he agreed to vouch for my qualifications.

RESULT: As a result of my experience and his recommendation, I was offered a train-the-trainer position. And that is how I began my career in coaching and mentoring teachers.

Question 48. Give an example of how you put the company's needs ahead of your career goals.

OBSTACLE: Because of financial reasons, the Merit Company downsized several departments. Afraid that their positions were in jeopardy, many co-workers embarked on job searches. Ultimately, a third of them offered their resignations within three months.

ACTION: On the other hand, I reaffirmed my commitment to the organization, and instead of looking for a new opportunity, I concentrated my efforts on ensuring that the company stayed afloat. This meant that I managed my tasks as well as took over the work of ex-employees. Without protesting, I tackled each assignment, bringing work home and working overtime when necessary.

RESULT: Though upper management continued its layoff efforts, my dedication to the company was recognized and I never received a pink slip. In fact, I survived several downsizing cycles. It was a bumpy few years, but the company made it through its economic crisis.

Question 49. Tell me about a time when you assumed a position or took on a task that was below your experience because you knew it would lead to better opportunities.

SITUATION: Though I had many years' experience running a small catering company, I was excited to learn of an opportunity to be a prep cook for the well-known organization Delectable Catering. Knowing that I would have to close down my company if I were to receive and accept the job offer, I applied for the position nonetheless because it would afford me access to high-end affairs with celebrities and politicians, where budget would be unimportant.

ACTION: After three rounds of interviews, the position was offered and I accepted. Without skipping a beat, I immersed myself in the kitchen, making recommendations for menus.

RESULT: Within a year I was charged with directing some of the company's major events. Through word-of-mouth, I was sought after by both new and existing clients. The referrals brought in a great deal of revenue for Delectable Catering, and as I suspected, the large-scale events were challenging, leaving me satisfied that I made the right move.

Question 50. Give me an example of how your first job prepared you for this one.

SITUATION: When I worked as a product demonstrator in a retail environment, I became accustomed to talking to complete strangers about product offerings.

ACTION: By engaging consumers and answering product-specific questions, I developed a strong ability to hold the customer's attention.

RESULT: Owing to that experience, I learned how to connect with customers instantly. This led to my success in securing profitable and sustainable relationships with clients.

Question 51. Tell me about the most competitive situation you have experienced and how you handled it.

SITUATION: When I was employed at Stone Imaging, I was in the running for a promotion; the other candidate was a colleague who was well liked and admired by many people in the company, myself included.

ACTION: I put together a proposal that highlighted the company's most important objectives for the first three months. Though this step was not required, or requested by management, I felt my initiative would give me a competitive edge.

RESULT: In the end, my colleague was awarded the promotion. However, a new position was created for me based on the proposal I had submitted. The outcome was a win-win situation for everyone involved.

Question 52. Provide an example of a real-life experience that prepared you for this position.

SITUATION: Sixteen years ago my son was born with autism.

ACTION: Since I knew nothing about the syndrome, I immersed myself in researching autism, so as to learn all I could about the condition. The information I gathered helped me in my development as a mother, and also in my dealings with the doctor.

RESULT: As part of that experience, I learned where to go and how to research a subject, quickly and thoroughly. My ability to research subjects quickly cuts down on preparation time for completing assignments. In addition, as my son's condition made his behavior unpredictable, I honed an ability to adapt my communication style to meet his varying needs. This flexible communication skill is useful when dealing with co-workers and clients.

Chapter **7**

Competency #2— Managerial/ Leadership Skills

Managing people to reach a common goal translates into high productivity and revenue levels for a business. This successful management is achieved through effective coaching and inspiring actions, whereby managers make employees feel valued and content at work. A great leader is able to take charge of a situation, assemble the necessary resources, and mobilize the staff. That leader will have a positive ripple effect on a department's success, increasing productivity many times over.

With so much at stake, businesses need management personnel who have strong leadership qualities. Accordingly, management-level candidates are assessed differently from other candidates. The core competencies that interviewers focus on for management candidates are leadership ability, employee motivation techniques, the ability to delegate, and strategic planning skills.

Leadership

Effective leadership positively impacts an organization in many ways (e.g., increases productivity, streamlines processes). Some questions asked during the interview will help the interviewer assess your ability to influence the direction of the department in which you are applying.

Career Values and Key Behaviors

A. Manages people. Can lead others and take control of projects while simultaneously maintaining quality standards, from inception of the project to its completion.

Example: _____

_____

_____

B. Praises good work. Takes the time to acknowledge employee efforts.

Example: _____

_____

_____

C. Has an open-door policy. Creates an atmosphere in which team members feel comfortable presenting their concerns.

Example: _____

_____

_____

D. A team builder. Nurtures an environment in which employees work together as a team to meet objectives.

Example: _____

_____

_____

E. A mentor. Serves as an adviser, successfully building individuals into top performers and groups as highly effective teams.

Example: _____

_____

_____

F. Strong inner resources. Has the strength of character to trust gut instincts and take the initiative to drive change.

Example: _____

_____

_____

G. **Charisma.** Displays a natural ability to captivate an audience and hold its interest; someone with a presence that commands respect.

Example: _____

_____

_____

H. **Professional integrity.** Understands the value of honesty, accountability, and trust in a business environment.

Example: _____

_____

_____

I. **Visionary.** An idea person who challenges traditional ways of conducting business and is willing to take calculated risks.

Example: _____

_____

_____

J. **Employee buy-in.** Demonstrates the ability to think strategically, act tactically, and motivate others to buy into new ideas, concepts, and values.

Example: _____

_____

_____

Questions and Answers

Question 53. Tell me about a time you reviewed someone else's work to ensure that quality standards were met.

SITUATION: When I worked for the Electronic Place, I found the marketing department staff were good wordsmiths. However, they did not have a grasp of the technical aspects of the company's offerings. Since I headed the technical department, it was up to me to collaborate with the marketing team and provide them with the information they needed to create magazine articles.

ACTION: During our discussions, I would break down complex technical subjects into easy-to-understand portions. I would use simple language instead of jargon. With the information I provided, they developed articles that I then proofed and edited before giving approval.

RESULT: The marketing department successfully placed their articles in trade publications, which in turn increased the company's presence in the marketplace.

Question 54. Not every employee is easygoing. There are times when an employee will refuse to carry out an order he or she believes is unfair. Please describe such a time and how you resolved the situation.

SITUATION: An employee insisted on carrying out only the responsibilities that were outlined in his job description. Whenever he was charged with an assignment not specifically mentioned in the job description, he refused to perform the task.

ACTION: To squash any misunderstanding about his functions, I explained that special duties assigned by the supervisor are permissible as long as the scope of that responsibility is within the classification of that position.

RESULT: After our meeting, the employee embraced the responsibilities assigned to him, seeing them as covered in his job description.

Question 55. Describe an occasion when you managed a situation that was out of the ordinary for your position.

SITUATION: We had a male employee who, after a long time of employment, revealed that she was transgender. She requested permission to come to work in women's clothing. In addition, she wanted the organization to have a sensitivity-training professional educate employees on how to deal with this new development.

ACTION: Without hesitation, I hired a consultant, who came in to offer staff training on how best to approach the situation sensitively.

RESULT: The training was interactive and helped everyone maintain an effective work environment. Ultimately, the fact that the employee was transgender never became an issue.

Question 56. Tell me about a time you implemented an initiative and met resistance from the majority of your staff.

SITUATION: At Autumn Affairs, person-to-person contacts and phone interactions between employees were minimal. For the most part, everyone relied on e-mail to communicate.

ACTION: To create a friendlier, more personalized work environment, I implemented a "no e-mail Friday," during which no one was allowed to use e-mail to contact individuals who were in the same building. Everyone was required to get up from his or her desk and speak to the co-worker in person. When the employees needed to communicate with others in another building or a different state, they were required to pick up the phone and call.

RESULT: The one-on-one interactions opened the door to friendships. Employees began to eat lunch together outside of the office and went for walks during their lunch break. This, in turn, increased team cohesiveness and productivity.

Question 57. Recall a time you were successful as a project leader.

SITUATION: At the Ingalls Company, I was assigned to lead marketing and advertising initiatives that encompassed conceptualizing and implementing an integrated marketing program for clients from a broad range of industries.

ACTION: As team leader, I managed a multimillion-dollar program and the launch of marketing campaigns under highly challenging conditions, including market-dominating competitors, downturned markets, and restricted budgets.

RESULT: Along with my team, we built a strong portfolio of quantifiable successes, with recent results including a 40 percent customer base increase for Comfy Slippers, a 68 percent return on investment for National Freights, and a $2 million revenue growth for Control Assets.

Question 58. Tell me about a time when you fired an employee whom you personally got along with.

SITUATION: Rebecca had a great personality and did a stellar job as a graphic designer. Clients raved about her work, but unfortunately she missed every other deadline. She claimed that it was because she was a perfectionist and did not want to submit work before it was finished. Because of her craftsmanship, I allowed her to set deadlines she could meet, as opposed to providing a timetable for her. Regrettably, she kept missing those deadlines as well.

ACTION: Since it is important to make a distinction between someone's personality and their performance on the job, I let her go. The termination did not come as a surprise to her, since we had had several performance-based conversations.

RESULT: Though terminating her employment was not a pleasant experience, my decision was sound and fair. Within a month of the firing, I hired a designer who was just as talented as Rebecca and who met her deadlines.

Question 59. Describe a time when a subordinate disagreed with a task he or she was given. How did you manage the situation?

SITUATION: The human resources director at the Lincoln Project wanted the department to create a "Pocket Employee Reference Guide." He believed that employees' easy access to policies and procedures would improve moral. The human resources generalist who was assigned the task felt that her time could be put to better use. She wanted me to speak to the director about the matter.

ACTION: I listened to her point of view and offered advice. I told her that it was important to choose one's battles carefully. This particular project was not one to fuss over, since the director had already made up his mind.

RESULT: In the end, she completed the pocket guide without expressing further discontent.

Question 60. Describe an occasion when you trained a cross-functional team.

SITUATION: Throughout my tenure with Ross Dress for Less, I led a cross-functional team that consistently achieved goals.

ACTION: To build upon the success, I introduced a new program that covered merchandising, operational management, and customer service.

RESULT: After I trained four store managers, two assistant managers, and two area supervisors, the store benefited from a boost in sales, productivity, and profitability.

Question 61. Give an example of a time when you took on a leadership role.

SITUATION: Within three months of employment with Dupree Company, I noticed that the teamwork was significantly less effective than at other organizations I worked for. The lack of collaboration negatively impacted the company's productivity.

ACTION: In order to boost working relationships, I volunteered to work overtime and without compensation to develop and implement a bi-weekly innovative education and training seminar for forty employees.

RESULT: Management green-lit my initiative. The result was that the program enhanced a team environment, where staff members came together to perform at a consistently high level.

Question 62. Tell me about a time when you brought two departments together to work effectively with each other.

OBSTACLE: When I worked for Gibson Music, the sales department had to meet quota, and they were overzealous in their efforts to land a contract. Many employees would overpromise and the technical department could not deliver.

ACTION: I instituted a culture in which the sales team did not feel pressured to close on deals at any cost. Instead, their sales pitch focused on addressing client needs and determining a package that met those needs while ensuring that the technical department could work within the parameters specified.

RESULT: I created synergy between the sales and technical departments, ensuring that strong communications between the two translated into top-notch customer experiences and increased profitability.

Question 63. Describe a time when a staff member did not meet your expectations, and what you did about it.

SITUATION: As a newly promoted manager for the Comic Strips Company, I met with an employee who was not meeting his goals. Upper management wanted me to let him go; however, I was hesitant because I wanted to see if he could thrive under my supervision.

ACTION: Before I gave him notice, I sat down with him to outline the areas he needed to improve. We then developed an action plan for how he could tackle each competency. Periodically, I asked about his progress and if he needed assistance. In addition, I always left my door open for questions.

Despite my efforts, he never asked for assistance and he continued to perform poorly.

RESULT: In the end, I fired him. Or, I should say, he fired himself because I gave him the opportunity to succeed.

Question 64. Give an example of a situation in which you changed the status quo in order to cultivate leaders.

SITUATION: The managers at National Stillwater promoted or praised employees who never ruffled feathers. They frequently overlooked employees who questioned procedures or offered suggestions for improvement—unfortunately, these people were usually labeled "difficult." From my point of view, that was a mistake. The managers needed to differentiate between doers and visionaries, and to promote accordingly.

ACTION: I instituted a training program that emphasized the characteristics and accomplishments that managers should search for when defining the leaders in their departments.

RESULT: The number of qualified leaders who moved up the corporate ladder grew as a result.

Question 65. Describe a time when you managed an individual who had excellent hard skills, but needed help with his or her soft skills.

OBSTACLE: A technician in my department was effective at his job. Unfortunately, before he attended to customer problems, he would provide the customers with ways they could have avoided the situation in the first place. Though that information was useful, the customers felt that he should first fix the problem and then lay out the details of how to avoid troubles in the future.

ACTION: I spoke with the technician and explained the situation while complimenting his hard skills.

RESULT: His work continued to be stellar, and at the same time the number of complaints I received decreased tremendously.

Employee Motivation

Employees are an organization's richest resource. Motivated teams lead to better results in the marketplace. As such, interviewers will ask questions to determine the methods you use to stimulate innovation in team members.

Career Value and Key Behaviors

A. **Trusting, engaging demeanor.** Employees view the leadership provided as a source of inspiration and encouragement.

Example: _____

_____

_____

B. **Leads by example.** Sets the pace and direction for employees to follow.

Example: _____

_____

_____

C. **Astute.** Has the ability to strike a balance between the needs of the organization and the needs of employees.

Example: _____

_____

_____

D. **Sets expectations.** Establishes shared values, gives clear guidelines, and provides direction to employees.

Example: _____

_____

_____

E. **Open communication.** Provides constructive feedback to stimulate employee output.

Example: _____

_____

_____

F.   **Keen people skills.** Able to identify and tap into the intrinsic motivations of employees.

Example: _____

_____

_____

G. **Motivator.** Creates an environment where employees feel empowered to perform at high levels.

Example: _____

_____

_____

H. **Creativity.** Brings out the best in people through the implementation of incentive programs.

Example: _____

_____

_____

I. **Facilitates cooperation.** Involves team members in decision-making processes and trusts their judgment to advance the departmental needs.

Example: _____

_____

_____

J. **Active listening.** Focuses on employee needs when they have work-related problems, listens, and offers guidance on how to handle negative situations.

Example: _____

_____

_____

Interview Questions and Answers

Question 66. Tell me about an occasion when you increased employee morale.

Situation: At AirTravel, productivity was at an all-time low. After several attempts to pinpoint the cause, we concluded that employees were receiving mixed messages on how to do their jobs. This was a result of departmental managers' consistently changing the work parameters. Though it is understandable that task specifications change from time to time, the rapid rate that these revisions were made bewildered the employees.

ACTION: To eliminate confusion, I introduced an employee evaluation process in which managers were to set measurable indicators and expectations before a project was begun. The managers were instructed not to change those specifications without carefully considering the ramifications.

RESULT: The new system improved employee performance and, in turn, revitalized management and staff relationships.

Question 67. Recall the last time you experienced low employee productivity. What was the situation and how did you handle it?

SITUATION: The Stewart & Marshall law firm had over a hundred and fifty attorneys and well over three hundred support staff. For reasons I am unsure of, there were no company-wide standard procedures for the paralegals. The lack of protocol led to inconsistent practices and low productivity levels.

ACTION: I established an internal group, called the Professional Paralegal Committee, whose members helped develop policies and procedures that focused on four key areas—service, excellence, practice, and leadership.

RESULT: The established guidelines provided continuity of work practices and increased the level of satisfaction of the firm's partners.

Question 68. Give an example of a time when your coaching efforts failed.

SITUATION: Seemingly out of nowhere, an employee's performance started to decline. This came as a shock, because a month earlier he had received high rankings on his review.

ACTION: Not one to let matters spiral out of control, I met with him to discuss ways he could get back on track. During our meeting he was distant; half the time I do not believe he was mentally present. I suggested he make use of the company's Employee Assistance Program to discuss matters with someone else, as he may not have been comfortable to share them with me.

RESULT: The employee refused to contact the EAP, and any effort that I made to reach out to him was met with resistance. As per standard procedure, I wrote him up whenever he strayed from company policy. Eventually, he resigned his position without a word as to the reason.

Question 69. Describe a time when you had to address a problem with an employee without alienating him or her.

Obstacle: When I came on board at Executive-Level Suites Company, I was told that a certain employee had many complaints against her for poor work performance. Her actions caused a rift among several departments. After gathering information regarding those past offenses, I realized that the problem was her inability to grasp how each department functioned independently but also as part of a team. So when she missed her deadline to provide Accounting with spreadsheets, this caused a backup in that department.

Action: As part of an initiative to bring her into the fold, and not target her specifically, I implemented a company-wide cross-training program that gave team members the opportunity to work in various departments.

Result: This approach served two purposes. First, the problem employee did not feel alienated and resent the training. Second, the initiative provided all employees with an opportunity to learn new skills and see how the departments are interconnected. This effort led to greater understanding of each division's specific needs and how lateness on a project, or not answering e-mails in a timely fashion, affected the progress of others.

Question 70. Describe a time when you provided one-on-one training support.

Situation: To cut down on costs, the management of New Horizon's Medical Facility decided to replace the registered nurse with a clerical team member. Since the clerk was unfamiliar with the intake process, the switch resulted in poorly completed intake forms and decreased patient conversion rate.

Action: During a one-month period, I created and executed a series of training sessions that focused on patient needs identification and follow-up strategies.

Result: The clerk's conversion rate increased by 40 percent shortly thereafter.

Question 71. Give an example of an innovative way that you promoted teamwork.

Situation: Though I did implement an employee rewards system to increase productivity, including providing financial bonuses for jobs well done, I thought it was a good idea to get the company involved in a nonprofit endeavor to increase team cohesiveness.

Action: I scouted options, e-mailed employees the mission statements of three viable charities, and asked them to vote on the organization they would like to support. After the votes were tallied, the Children's Lending Library program was the clear winner. The charity focuses on providing schools in Latin America with libraries. As part of the initiative, employees could choose to donate books and /or volunteer to sort and mail the books right before the holiday season.

Result: A few months later, we received cards and photos from the school we "adopted." The book drive was such a hit with the employees that it became an annual event.

Question 72. Describe the last training workshop you led.

Situation: As the account manager for Sounds in Motion, I traveled across the country to train channel partners on the benefits of our products. However, there came a time when the business grew to the point where I was stretched too thin and training was backed up for months.

Action: Taking advantage of today's technology, I developed interactive Web-based modules on market opportunities, sales promotions, customer objections, and the manufacturer's product features and benefits.

Result: These "webinars" offered great flexibility on dates, contained costs, and provided channel partners with training that could be repeated as many times as they wished. This in turn increased sales and expanded the channel partners' knowledge of our products.

Question 73. Describe a time when you were responsible for making drastic changes in your department while at the same time had to minimize employees' negative reactions.

Situation: Horseshoe Productions was hit hard by the sluggish economy. To keep our head above water, I implemented initiatives to reduce costs.

Action: I determined that the best way to approach the cuts was to engage employees, asking them to suggest ways the department could trim waste.

RESULT: This decision worked to the organization's advantage, since employees took ownership of the proposed cuts. Consequently, the team rallied around the organization's revitalization efforts, and not one employee complained about the changes.

Question 74. Tell me about a time when you trained an employee to do his or her job better.

SITUATION: At St. Mary's Medical Center, we had a problem with an employee who did not follow company procedures on a regular basis. She was approached informally by management to resolve the situation, but because Human Resources was afraid she would file a lawsuit for age discrimination, she was never formally reprimanded. Her actions and the organization's inaction escalated the issue.

ACTION: After checking her annual reviews, I realized that she had a stellar track record for years and that her performance started to decline when new management took over. Upon further investigation, it was clear that her decline came after many of her responsibilities were assigned to others. From my point of view, it seemed that she no longer felt valued as a team member and as a result her work began to suffer. To increase her motivation, I encouraged the department head to offer her complete ownership of an upcoming project.

RESULT: The employee felt empowered, and completed the project effectively. Over time she was rewarded for her revitalized work ethic by being given more projects to lead.

Question 75. Describe a time when you realized that a top producer on your team was growing bored with his or her position. What did you do about it?

SITUATION: Robert, a sales executive with year after year of quota-surpassing performance, began to show signs of discontentment. Though his sales remained high, his enthusiasm for the job had waned.

ACTION: I approached management about penetrating the northeast region, where Robert could serve as the regional sales manager.

RESULT: Management and Robert embraced the challenge. His interest in the company was restored. With Robert's newfound energy, he successfully developed the talents and strengths of his team, motivating each to attain high performance targets.

Question 76. As much as we may try to get along with everyone else, there are occasions when we cannot. Describe a time when you managed an employee with whom you did not see eye-to-eye.

SITUATION: We hired an employee who operated his own business for fifteen years. Since he was used to running the show for so many years, he did not take direction well.

ACTION: I decided to deal with the behavior, not the person. During a meeting, I focused on his performance on the job. Together we developed a behavior-modification plan.

RESULT: After a few months, he decided to take another stab at starting his own business. However, we did part as friends.

Question 77. We all have outside interests. Tell me about an extracurricular activity you enjoy. Then describe a time when the skills you learned in that activity made you a better professional.

SITUATION: I serve as a defensive player for a volleyball team. The spirit of competition, including the importance of leaving negative feelings on the court, spills over into my work environment. This attitude was useful the day I overheard a colleague downplay my role in the execution of a major project.

ACTION: While my colleague was talking, I paid attention to the director's body language. He was clearly uncomfortable with the conversation. When I had the opportunity to speak to him privately, I emphasized the actions I had implemented while also noting that all members of the team contributed to the success of the project.

RESULT: Though I am sure many factors came into play, I believe my professionalism was an integral reason I was offered leadership of the next project.

Ability to Delegate

A strong ability to delegate effectively will ensure that projects are completed on time and within scope. To measure your experience in assigning projects, a subset of questions asked during the interview will focus on delegation.

Career Values and Key Behaviors

A. **Sets clear expectations.** Provides employees with guidelines to complete tasks efficiently while maintaining open lines of communications to ensure ongoing success.

Example: _____

_____

_____

B. **Assesses employee skills.** Takes into account the employee's strengths and weaknesses and assigns projects accordingly.

Example: _____

_____

_____

C. **Instills employee trust.** Notifies an employee of the task and lets him or her choose the best path to completion.

Example: _____

_____

_____

D. **Provides support.** Praises good work publicly and addresses problems privately.

Example: _____

_____

_____

E. **Promotes advancement.** Encourages employees to step up and volunteer for tasks that are in need of delegation.

Example: _____

_____

_____

F. **Manages time.** Determines which activities are the best use of one's own time and assigns the remaining initiatives to others.

Example: _____

_____

_____

G. **Acts as a mentor.** Trusts employees to solve their own problems, providing suggestions only when asked.

Example: _____

_____

_____

H. **Assigns responsibly.** Delegates conscientiously and maintains control over projects that one has expertise in.

Example: _____

_____

_____

I. **Promotes cooperation.** Designates committees to work on projects and reinforces collaborative teamwork.

Example: _____

_____

_____

J. **Trusts employee commitments.** Leaves employees to their own devices and avoids questioning or second-guessing their progress once the tasks are delegated.

Example: _____

_____

_____

Interview Questions and Answers

Question 78. Describe a time when you entrusted a subordinate with an activity that he or she did not complete.

OBSTACLE: I assigned a newly hired assistant the task of developing a PowerPoint presentation for the director who was scheduled to speak at a convention. After the assistant completed the presentation, I reviewed it to evaluate its quality. Regrettably, I noted it needed a revamp because it used old-school methods—the images were outdated, the bulleted statements were too long.

ACTION: Knowing that the director could not present the material in its current condition, I met with the assistant to discuss the required changes.

RESULT: Together we worked on the project until every detail met the director's standards. And since the assistant's knowledge of PowerPoint was limited, I enrolled her in a class to update her skills.

Question 79. Tell me about a time when you delegated work to a group.

SITUATION: As a certified public accountant for Tax Preparation Corporation, I prepared taxes, audits, and financial statements for clients in various industries, including construction, fashion, financial institutions, real estate, and health care.

ACTION: To streamline the processes, I assigned employees to teams so they could manage accounts within the same industry.

RESULTS: The effort increased client relationships, simplified billing, and slashed tax preparation turnaround.

Question 80. Describe a time when you divided the responsibilities of a task to members of a group.

SITUATION: As an account supervisor for a large PR firm, I implemented a community affairs program in a short amount of time that was intended to educate the public about a new initiative our client was launching. The project was funded through a grant, so it all had to be managed well.

ACTION: I assembled a team of four and had each one handle a specific aspect of the program. One person handled media; one a mailing—which included working with a production team; one person spent time identifying community organizations; and another person focused on putting together a list of local elected officials.

RESULT: Delegating the tasks was the best way to obtain information about every aspect of the project; I could then report back to my superiors, and consequently, to our client. The employees took ownership of their responsibilities, forged their own relationships, and helped the successful launch of the campaign.

Question 81. Tell me about a time when you delegated a project to a junior staff member because you realized you had too much on your plate.

Situation: I was the editor of a leisure/entertainment/recreation magazine. We needed to compile a restaurant directory for a region that included more than six thousand restaurants. I believed that developing a strong restaurant directory was key to success for the magazine, as I found that most—if not all—of the current restaurant directories serving the region were less than adequate. I originally thought I had to take on the task myself, for two reasons. First, I was the only one who understood what a real restaurant directory should be, and second, I was the only one crazy enough to care that all restaurants were adequately represented.

Action: I decided to delegate the job because I just did not have the time to tackle the project. About the same time, however, I realized that the newly hired assistant editor was very responsible and was the perfect choice to take on the task.

Result: The assistant editor embraced the opportunity, making the directory into something even better than I could have hoped for.

Question 82. Recall an occasion when you got bogged down in a task's details instead of giving the job to someone else.

Situation: I was the director of special projects for an entrepreneur who was involved in a lot of community projects. One of those projects was running a breakfast event that was attended by the presidents of local chambers of commerce and elected officials. Obviously there was a great deal of protocol and exacting procedures to be followed.

Action: After getting bogged down in the minutia of who had to sit where and what order people were to be introduced, I decided to focus instead on my boss's role at the breakfast meeting and let my assistant do all the seat placement and agenda coordination.

Result: I was able to focus on the big picture and not worry about the details. In the end, the breakfast went off without a hitch.

Question 83. Give an example of a time when you delegated a task and, in the middle of the project, the employee asked you to take it over.

Situation: Because there was a lien on a client's mortgage, she was unable to sell her home. Two things complicated the matter. First, the client indicated she had paid the debt but did not have a copy of the satisfaction letter. Second, the creditor closed its doors several years ago. Since it would take a lot of research to track down the file, I assigned the task to a legal assistant. Several times the assistant expressed concern about the difficulties she was encountering. Though she did not come right out and ask me, all indications pointed to her wanting me to intervene.

ACTION: Though I didn't offer to take over the work, I did offer advice on the steps to take. It was important that she learn to manage difficult situations such as these on her own.

RESULT: It took her two weeks longer than I expected to complete the task, but she did locate the necessary letter.

Question 84. Describe a time when you assigned a project to an employee and dealt with the reactions of those who were passed over.

SITUATION: As the vice president of communications for the Medium Collective, I assigned a lucrative project to Yvette, an employee who had joined the team only a month earlier. My decision ruffled a few feathers among the high producers, as they felt the decision should have been based on seniority. I understood their point, and there were times when I took seniority into consideration. This time, however, I felt that Yvette's accomplishments with previous companies outshone the best employees on Medium's payroll. Since she was the most qualified, she received the opportunity.

ACTION: When approached by staff members about my decision, I provided an honest assessment of the situation. Given that I have solid working relationships with the team members and have earned their respect, there was no fallout—only genuine curiosity.

RESULT: Yvette delivered exceptional results. The next lucrative project that came our way, I assigned to another team member—as it is my philosophy that all members share in the opportunities to tackle challenging assignments.

Question 85. Tell me about a time when you provided instructions for doing a task and an employee offered a smarter alternative.

SITUATION: Many employees had questions regarding their health-care and life insurance benefits. Given that, I suggested to the benefits coordinator that he hold a meeting to answer questions. Since he has more employee interactions than I do, he informed me that the overwhelmingly majority of male employees mentioned that their wives made the benefits decisions. He proposed holding the gathering on a weekend to allow spouses to attend.

ACTION: As he suggested, the meeting was held to a packed audience on a Saturday afternoon.

RESULT: During the presentation, he answered questions and calls to the office regarding company benefits dramatically decreased as a consequence.

Question 86. Give an example of a time when you delegated a task because you did not want to do it yourself.

SITUATION: Regardless of the task involved, each project for which I am accountable requires the same focus and dedication.

ACTION: With that in mind, I never pawn off my responsibilities to employees. I have too much respect for their time. Instead, when there is a task that I can't get excited about, I work on it right away.

RESULT: Doing so allows me to complete the task quickly, check it off my list, and concentrate on activities that I find more gratifying.

Question 87. Recall a time when you asked for employee feedback before delegating tasks.

SITUATION: To determine a clerical employee's interests, I asked about her immediate and long-term career goals. She indicated that her passion was for employee development and training.

ACTION: Based on this information, I gave her the go-ahead to provide the training that was a small section of the new employee orientation program.

RESULT: She soon advanced to creating training catalogs and then to developing tutorials and manuals on how to use computer applications.

Question 88. Describe an occasion when you divided the functions of a team among its members.

SITUATION: At Uniform Exchange, the online sales cycle was longer than management was comfortable with.

ACTION: In an effort to close sales at a faster pace, I sourced and implemented online chat software that allowed agents to invite visitors to communicate in real time. I split the agents into two categories: one group dealt with phone inquiries and the other was trained in chat communications.

RESULT: The solution shortened the sales cycle. An added benefit was that the software tracked the Web pages visitors read and how long they spent on each page. I used the new intelligence to revamp the content of our pages to include an assertive sales pitch that went for the close.

Strategic Planning

Strategic planning serves as a vehicle for a company's calculated growth. Interviewers will gauge the steps you take to develop an action plan that will take an organization from A to Z.

Career Values and Key Behaviors

A. **Creates a roadmap.** Develops and implements calculated procedures for success.

Example: _____

_____

_____

B. **Does SWOT analysis.** Identifies Strengths, Weaknesses, Opportunities, and Threats when determining what measures to use in solving a problem.

Example: _____

_____

_____

C. **Develops relationships.** Cultivates and nurtures strategic partnerships to open new channels of business.

Example: _____

_____

_____

D. **Defines projects.** Develops a clear, purposeful game plan.

Example: _____

_____

_____

E. **Streamlines processes.** Clarifies expectations and routinely checks on progress to ensure successful completion of plans.

Example: _____

_____

_____

F. **Develops strategies.** Devises step-by-step strategies, encompassing actions and recognizing potential obstacles.

Example: _____

_____

_____

G. **Offers team support.** Provides the resources and guidance needed to achieve execution of established goals.

Example: _____

_____

_____

H. **Uses tactical planning.** Carries out the project's scope in order to gain a competitive advantage in key areas.

Example: _____

_____

_____

I. **Is inclusive.** Integrates the ideas of team members, considers market conditions, and aligns organizational objectives with the plan.

Example: _____

_____

_____

J. **Monitors the plan.** Evaluates the situation to determine whether plans need to be revised or changed.

Example: _____

_____

_____

Interview Questions and Answers

Question 89. Tell me about an important event you managed from beginning to end.

Situation: As an independent contractor, I plan an annual wine-tasting fund-raiser for a local charity.

Action: I single-handedly manage everything that needs to be done, from creating press kits that communicate key message points to handling the logistics of the event, to providing on-site hosting.

Result: Since the fund-raiser draws celebrities and public figures, the event garners national media attention. In turn, this attention translates into worldwide visits to the charity's Web site, where online contributions make up 25 percent of annual donations.

Question 90. Give an example of a time when your strategic planning skills came in handy.

Situation: Greenvale Studios staff was going through a transition, during which its corporate brand was diminishing. I was recruited to implement a strategy that would revitalize the Studio's position in the market.

Action: The first order of business was to put together a focus group to determine the positive and negative impressions of our products. Once we had the results, I met with the advertising department to brainstorm ideas for updating the products' images and redesign the marketing to appeal to new consumers.

Result: The process of rebranding takes time, but incrementally the organization started to rebound.

Question 91. Describe an occasion when you were charged with planning a company event.

Situation: When I was employed with Knots Landing Properties, the owners wanted to implement a measure that would position the company as a good corporate citizen that took an active interest in the community's growth.

Action: To attract business leaders to an event that would call attention to the company, I suggested a golf outing, with proceeds allocated for a scholarship fund for students majoring in business administration. The owners embraced the idea, and I was charged with handling the logistics, including negotiations with the facility where the event was to take place.

Result: Over the years, this golf match has become the go-to event of the summer and draws over one thousand participants.

Question 92. Tell me about a time when you partnered with another department to execute a plan.

Situation: As a strategic pricing manager for Knoxville Ventures, it was my role to mitigate pricing problems and capitalize on pricing opportunities.

Action: I collaborated with the marketing department to determine our products' attributes and our competitors' strengths and weaknesses, so as to determine the proper price point.

Result: Based on the information we gathered, I developed a monetary value that increased Knoxville's revenue by 15 percent.

Question 93. Describe an occasion when using strategic partners benefited the company's bottom line.

Situation: As the associate director for the real estate finance division for Luxurious Commercial Properties, my oversight responsibilities included structuring, analyzing, negotiating, and financing plans for housing projects and programs.

Action: I have been in this business long enough to have developed strategic relationships with equity partners, third-party developers, bankers, and underwriters. Consequently, I leveraged those relationships to negotiate better loan terms.

Result: While employed with Luxurious Commercial Properties, every loan I worked on closed. This is an unprecedented feat in the company's history.

Question 94. Describe a scenario when you helped a stagnant idea become a full-fledged plan.

SITUATION: The owners of FabricColors wanted to take their online endeavor up a notch by collaborating with a Yahoo! Online store. This was a project the owners mentioned frequently, but never followed through on.

ACTION: I took the initiative to source a Web designer with experience in creating a Yahoo! Store and I inquired how FabricColors' existing Web site could be enhanced. Together, we came up with a strategy and structure to ensure an engaging visitor experience.

RESULT: The inclusion of the Yahoo! Store platform made it easier for visitors to pay for items online. In turn, the company's profits soared.

Question 95. Give an example of a problem or situation that needed an immediate, short-term solution.

SITUATION: At McGruff and Sons, we had an old and rundown server. Every couple of days, I would receive an error message about a hardware failure. Replacement would cost over $8,000 and the company budget was already overstretched.

ACTION: I rebuilt a machine I had at home and brought it into the office to use until the department could afford a new one.

RESULT: The overhauled server held up for close to three years. When the new one was purchased, I was able to transfer all the data without any hiccups.

Question 96. Recall a time when you developed a mission statement.

SITUATION: *Play Book Magazine* did not institute a mission statement at its inception, so when I joined the publication, I took on the project.

ACTION: To get the employees involved, I asked for their input. Specifically, I asked them to describe *Play Book* in their own words and to e-mail me their thoughts. Based on the responses, I developed three statements that employees could vote on.

RESULT: The statement the company settled on was: "We keep sports lovers educated by providing them with entertaining, up-to-date information."

Question 97. Tell me about a time when your budget ran on a deficit. What were the circumstances?

SITUATION: When the economy took a downturn, sales at Matrix Solutions suffered an all-time low.

ACTION: I immediately sent a memo to the staff, outlining my directives to cut costs, including encouraging executives to fly coach, limiting lunch expenses, and eliminating client gifts. In addition, I set up an emergency meeting with the sales, marketing, and advertising teams to come up with recession-proof solutions.

RESULT: Considering the worldwide financial crisis at the time, and the numerous companies that had to downsize, Matrix fared well, since the deficit was only 4 percent.

Question 98. Describe a time when you questioned the direction your employer was taking. What was the result?

SITUATION: White Stripe is a small company. A family-like sense of camaraderie can be both an asset and a catalyst for nonprofessional behavior. This is due, in large part, to the absence of a human resources department.

ACTION: At my suggestion, the company hired an HR consultant to establish policies and manage functions, including employee relations, benefits, and compensation.

RESULT: The HR consultant had the team complete a 360-degree feedback assessment. The evaluation allowed us to rate each other in several categories. Through the evaluation, we learned how we are viewed by our peers. This insight paved the way for the team to raise the level of professionalism at the company. In turn, productivity and morale increased.

Question 99. Give an example of a situation in which you implemented a plan that had long-range implications.

SITUATION: In all my years of managing others, I have learned that, instead of guessing at what motivates employees, it is best to ask. I have also found that the best way to gain insight is to conduct surveys. One particular time, the overwhelming majority of staff members wanted the financial compensation model revisited.

ACTION: As a result of employee feedback, I substituted the seniority-based bonus policy with a pay-for-skill program whereby employees received monetary incentives for learning new activities and/or performing additional tasks.

RESULT: Management and employees raved about the new program. Employee productivity went through the roof, and revenue growth skyrocketed.

Question 100. Provide an example of your existing (previous) company's weakness and the steps you took to overcome it.

SITUATION: Omaha Management wanted to be all things to all customers. Unfortunately, this plan was not working; we could not identify and reach a niche market.

ACTION: In order to target specific customers, I implemented a plan that focused on supply-chain management and on retaining low prices on high-volume products.

RESULT: The efforts successfully brought in the lower- to middle-income customers whom we targeted. This established a recognizable brand and increased profits.

Question 101. Describe a time when your opinion on an operational matter differed from that of management.

SITUATION: Recruiting and training new employees takes a toll on a company's bottom line. Base Manufacturers wanted to eliminate turnover completely or at least get the percentage close to zero. Consequently, management stressed the importance of a low turnover rate, and supervisors felt compelled to keep low producers on staff. Though I understand the importance of keeping turnover low, it should not come at a cost of weak productivity.

ACTION: I proposed that management focus their efforts on instituting exit interviews to identify the reasons employees left or were terminated. Pinpointing the root cause, whether it was poor management or recruitment skills, was a sensible solution to solving the turnover problem.

RESULT: For about a year, the turnover rate hit peeks and valleys, until HR was able to uncover the reason for the high rate. The problem was in poor candidate screenings. A plan was put into place to better screen applicants and, as a result, turnover leveled off to a tolerable average.

Question 102. Tell me about a time when you consulted with a client to ensure that a project went smoothly.

SITUATION: As the lead project manager for Financial Enterprises, I implemented a software program to identify underperforming funds and to broaden diversification for Fortune 500 companies.

ACTION: I triaged client problems that occurred in the implementation process, including analyzing, determining specifications, and applying resolutions for every glitch.

RESULT: Owing to my customer service and technical proficiencies, I was awarded greater responsibilities during my tenure with the company, and I received numerous bonuses.

Question 103. Describe a time when you worked as part of an integrated team to come up with a plan of action.

SITUATION: As the educator for oncology nurses, I served on an integrated Regulatory Compliance Committee, which included doctors and specialists.

ACTION: During the meetings, we reviewed the findings of key reports that characterized the diverse needs of cancer survivors and outlined the guidelines for care.

RESULT: To optimize the facility's services, we developed policies and procedures for the safe delivery of inpatient and outpatient care, as well as house-wide guidelines for the safe handling of hazardous drugs.

Competency #3— Personal Motivation

Since enthusiasm is linked to goal attainment and increased performance, the ability to do the job takes a backseat to motivation and the eagerness to succeed. Interviewers understand that zeal is the first step toward ingenuity, which in turn contributes to an environment where ideas flourish and positive energy is contagious. Therefore, as an applicant looking for employment, you need to display enthusiasm for your work and welcome competency-based questions that allow you to give evidence of that enthusiasm.

From the employers' point of view, people who drag their feet are a demoralizing presence in an office and that kind of attitude can spread like wildfire through a business. Interviewers are looking to avoid hiring persons whose attitudes and behaviors will drag down everyone else. So, questions regarding your ambitions and examples of taking the initiative will come up during the interview.

Ambition

Interviewers understand that ambition is closely followed by success. As a result, they will ask questions to determine your level of determination to do what needs to be done in order to promote the organization's expansion.

Career Values and Key Behaviors

A. **Strives for accomplishment.** Shows an ability to outline a plan, determine a strategy, and set the wheels in motion in order to accomplish measurable goals.

Example: _____

_____

_____

B. **Demonstrates drive.** Displays a commitment to succeed in spite of all obstacles.

Example: _____

_____

_____

C. **Shows persistence.** Able to find alternatives when encountering stumbling blocks.

Example: _____

_____

_____

D. **Has aspirations.** Continuously searches for ways to grow professionally.

Example: _____

_____

_____

E. **Is resolute.** Has unshakeable determination to go all-out for what is desired.

Example: _____

_____

_____

F. **Is goal oriented.** Does not give way to pressures and continues to focus on the behaviors and thoughts that bring about necessary change.

Example: _____

_____

_____

G. **Is a life-long learner.** Continues to acquire mastery of new fields; promotes self-advancement and professional growth through personal development.

Example: _____

_____

_____

H. **Is level headed.** Balances passion and common sense to achieve goals.

Example: _____

_____

_____

I. **Shows commitment.** Demonstrates belief in an organization's mission and aspires to grow within the company.

Example: _____

_____

_____

J. **Has enthusiasm.** Draws energy from a love of the work and uses passion to produce stellar results.

Example: _____

_____

_____

Interview Questions and Answers

Question 104. Tell me about a time when you set and achieved a goal.

SITUATION: I applied to the Reliant Company because of its fine reputation for promoting from within. With my determination to go above and beyond what is expected of me, I hoped that soon after I was hired, I would be offered a promotion.

ACTION: Within my first week of employment, I set up a meeting with the department head for the purpose of developing a list of objectives that were important to achieve within a three-month period. We came up with three action items and created a plan for achieving each.

RESULT: For my three-month review, I drew up a checklist of the measures I had achieved, along with key ideas to enhance the department's productivity. My efforts and ideas garnered a promotion within a year's time.

Question 105. Recall a situation when you took on a self-starter approach to a project.

SITUATION: When I was hired as an assistant for Editorial Secrets, I searched for ways to carve a niche for myself. Concurrently, I took pride in performing the tasks that were listed in my job description, including taking minutes during departmental meetings.

ACTION: From those meetings I learned a lot about writing copy for brochures and Web sites. Occasionally, I would take it upon myself to write some copy and compare it to the final product developed by the copywriter. Through this exercise I learned about the skills in which I excelled and what I needed to improve.

RESULT: Over time, I had a portfolio of ads I had written and I showed it to the department head. She assigned me a small project, which was sent directly to the client. The client was impressed with the material, and after a while I was assigned more complex projects.

Question 106. Describe a time when you chose a course of action that had a significant impact on your career.

SITUATION: When I graduated from college I wanted to work in the industrial design department of the Lion Plant Company because the organization's international reputation as an industry leader was well known. Unfortunately, there were no positions open in my department of choice.

ACTION: I applied for the only open position, which was in the mailroom, anticipating that when a position became available as a designer, I could submit an application.

RESULT: It turned out that I enjoyed the camaraderie in the mailroom. My desire for industrial design took a backseat to the mailroom's departmental concerns. When the mailroom manager retired, I took over his position and worked my way up to an even higher position.

Question 107. Describe your most recent achievement and explain how your actions benefited investors.

SITUATION: I negotiated the acquisition of The Summit, a failing company, from private equity investors.

ACTION: As part of the process, I drafted the new business plan, led investor presentations, and negotiated equity financing from an investment firm.

RESULT: Within a year, I returned the company to profitability and positive cash flow.

Question 108. Give an example of a situation in which you discovered a flaw in operations. What did you do about it?

SITUATION: After reviewing recent purchases, I noticed that all the special orders were acquired through a preferred vendor, even when another vendor sold the same make and model at half the cost.

ACTION: I spoke to members of the purchasing department to determine their reasoning behind such purchases. It came to my attention that the head of purchasing had mandated that all special orders be acquired through a specific vendor. I changed the policy to reflect policies that made sense to the department's bottom line.

RESULT: Purchasing costs significantly decreased, as happens with competitive bidding.

Question 109. Recall a time when your performance on the job led to greater responsibility.

SITUATION: As an office manager, I was successful in targeting inefficiencies that negatively impacted the bottom line. Based on the results my efforts garnered, management assigned me to a special project that entailed reengineering processes regionally.

ACTION: In each office, I retrained the low producers on various competencies, including customer service, sales, and account management.

RESULT: All divisions enjoyed an increase in profits and customer satisfaction.

Question 110. Describe a time when you did not know a problem existed until it was brought to your attention.

OBSTACLE: At Colby's Place, we had dedicated volunteers who visited AIDS/HIV patients. Unfortunately, we received many complaints from the volunteers that the patients they were assigned frequently were not at home for their scheduled visits. As a result, many volunteers dropped out of the program as they felt their time was not being respected.

ACTION: I developed a training program for the AIDS/HIV patients that stressed the collaborative relationship between them and their sponsors. I pointed out that Colby's Place expected volunteers to keep their commitments to patients, and patients also had a responsibility to the volunteers.

RESULT: The program strengthened after this understanding was reached, and we received an influx of both volunteers and patients. Increased numbers then led to more donations and more community recognition.

Question 111. Give an example of an occasion when your job became mundane and what you did to make the time pass more quickly.

SITUATION: The Google ads we used at Shingles Roofing were a success; my responsibility was simply to monitor the ads and make adjustments when necessary. Over time, the ads became self-sustaining, so I began to look for ways to target a new demographic. Since the Hispanic population is growing steadily in the United States, I wrote ads in Spanish.

ACTION: Using the Keyword Chaser software, I prepared a list of new words to target. Then I wrote the corresponding ads to show my supervisor.

RESULT: During the next budget meeting, money was allocated for the ads I had created. Out of five new ads, four brought in additional revenue.

Question 112. Tell me about a time when you were proud of your efforts. What were the circumstances?

SITUATION: As the director of technology for Sayville Medical Center, I was recruited to improve workplace efficiencies, optimize business processes, and standardize systems.

ACTION: As a course of action, I revamped help-desk policies and procedures to ensure courteous, timely, and effective resolution of end-user problems. Once the new procedures were in place, I instituted weekly meetings at which time employees were held accountable for the department's successes and failures.

RESULT: Within three months, I reorganized a dysfunctional technical department into a team-focused service-delivery organization in which all end-user expectations were met.

Question 113. Describe a time when you requested help or assistance on a project or assignment.

SITUATION: At the Agency Group, files were split among agents. I was responsible for clients whose last names began with *K* through *O*. When hurricane Zachary hit Florida, we had many claims, the majority of which were my responsibility to process.

ACTION: During my co-workers downtime I asked for their assistance. We were a close-knit group and everyone helped me process the backlog of claims.

RESULT: Without having to work overtime, all the necessary paperwork was completed without errors.

Question 114. Give an example of a situation in which you demonstrated your willingness to work hard.

SITUATION: I worked for a mom-and-pop shop that had a primitive accounting system, in which all activities were logged in an old-fashioned ledger book.

ACTION: I wanted to learn QuickBooks, but the owners could not afford the software and training. On freebarter.com, I found an older version of the software. A friend of mine used QuickBooks at her job, and I asked if she could show me the ins and outs of the program. She agreed, and we met several times after work or on the weekends.

RESULT: After a few weeks, I learned how to use the system and I streamlined the accounting practice for my employer.

Question 115. Describe an occasion when you made a difficult choice between your personal and your professional life.

SITUATION: After many years of working for corporate America, I longed for an opportunity to live outside of the United States. I was hesitant because my career was on an upswing, and taking time from my job was risky. But the nagging feeling would not go away. It got to the point where I could not ignore the urge.

ACTION: I requested a sabbatical from my employer, obtained a Switzerland working visa, and applied for a position as a guide for the Switzerland Museum of History.

RESULT: I educated visitors about the artwork in the museum. After work, I enjoyed the Swiss culture and its people. I returned to the States revitalized, ready to tackle the challenges that lie ahead.

Question 116. Tell me about a time you leveraged contacts to meet a business goal.

SITUATION: As a television producer, it is important that I maintain solid relationships with political figures, both local and national. Recently a story broke concerning a group of senators who had vowed to block a deal with a foreign entity unless the price of oil was stabilized.

ACTION: Since it was a newsworthy story I had difficulty contacting a member of the senate team, so I called in a favor to an oil lobbyist to see if he could arrange a meeting with the politicians involved.

RESULT: Every news department was after the story, but I got there first. Eventually they learned the details, however, our news team covered it as "breaking news."

Initiative

During a career, there are times to be a follower and other times when it's important to take the initiative. Taking the lead when necessary is an attribute that interviewers will focus on during an interview.

Career Values and Key Behaviors

A. **Proactive.** Anticipates problems and determines a tactical strategy to prevent issues from arising.

Example: _____

_____

_____

B. **Undertakes assignments.** Seeks out unfinished tasks and takes the proper steps to ensure their completion.

Example: _____

_____

_____

C. **Introduces cutting-edge ideas.** Keeps up to date on industry trends and uses emerging technologies for the betterment of the organization.

Example: _____

_____

_____

D. **Maintains continued interest.** Works through later challenges with the same vigor as at the beginning.

Example: _____

_____

_____

E. **Shows a can-do attitude.** Searches for ways to improve systems and change the status quo.

Example: _____

_____

_____

F. **Has leadership qualities.** Takes hold of a project or of people, providing the guidance or direction required to complete a task.

Example: _____

_____

_____

G. **Displays fortitude.** Has strong determination to confront problems with a resilience peppered with flexibility.

Example: _____

_____

_____

H. **Introspective.** Reflects upon past experiences and applies what was learned to ensure the success of current tasks.

Example: _____

_____

_____

I. **Purposeful.** Sets one's mind to completing a project, regardless of problems.

Example: _____

_____

_____

J. **Takes action.** Ready to initiate action without hesitation.

Example: _____

_____

_____

Interview Questions and Answers

Question 117. Recall a time when you were given a set of instructions that you were unable to follow.

SITUATION: When I first joined the Trading Company, I thought it was a sign of weakness to acknowledge that I didn't grasp a concept and needed clarification. This mind-set led to my struggling on a project and spending more time on it than necessary. I met the deadline, but only by a hair.

ACTION: For the next task assigned to me, I asked questions until I understood the project's scope and the steps I needed to take to complete it.

RESULT: I was able to finish my projects without feeling undue pressure. In addition, by asking questions of others, I built rapport with my co-workers.

Question 118. Give an example of a situation in which you did something that you knew had little chance of success.

SITUATION: In searching for ways to save the company money, I discovered that many offices were going paperless.

ACTION: I researched several software applications and identified the one that best fit the organization's needs. My research showed me, however, that the software license made the idea cost-prohibitive.

RESULT: Nevertheless, since I took the time to conduct the research, I submitted my findings to my immediate supervisor. She was so impressed not only with my initiative but also with the idea of going green. She forwarded the research to the head of the company. As I suspected, the licensing fees were out of reach, however, the company implemented the change a few years later in a satellite office. Eventually, the process was applied company-wide.

Question 119. Describe an occasion when an idea you had was met with enthusiasm by management.

SITUATION: The manual system for recording employee participation in training programs was cumbersome.

ACTION: I implemented a learning-management system whereby employees could register for courses, view a history of courses they had taken, receive reminders of upcoming workshops, and notify supervisors when the staff registered for courses. In addition, I created an e-mail announcement for the system, developed a tutorial with step-by-step instructions on how to use it, and offered training workshops.

RESULT: Since Human Resources was no longer required to provide employees with a list of training programs, their time was freed up to attend to more important departmental matters.

Question 120. Describe a time when you took an active role in a project for which you had little experience.

SITUATION: I worked as an administrative assistant for years. Though I had no experience, when the position of special communications specialist opened up, management approached me to consider it.

ACTION: I suggested and then launched a new intranet Web site to promote an Executive Briefing Program on a cross-company basis.

RESULT: The efforts resulted in 50 percent greater participation from all levels of management. The initiative also generated internal strategic partnerships based on improved interdepartmental communications.

Question 121. Give me an example of a time you worked for a startup.

SITUATION: Because it would be a challenge, I decided to work for a startup company that was obtaining a patent for LCD displays in elevators.

ACTION: I set up a client list of potential customers, and I introduced the idea of elevator commercial placements to the executives.

RESULT: Though I was successful in selling the product, unfortunately the patent was not approved and the operation shut down. That said, the experience I garnered, including how to expand territory and handle consulta-tive sales, was instrumental in my later success as an account executive.

Question 122. Recall a life-altering event that impacted your career choices.

SITUATION: It was not in my nature to take risks, in either my personal or my professional life. For instance, I never competed with co-workers on challenging projects. Usually I sat by the sidelines and waited for manage-ment to assign me a task. Unexpectedly, my father passed away in a car crash. I thought about the sacrifices he had made for our family to ensure we succeeded in life.

ACTION: I decided to quit my job and enroll in an MBA program.

RESULT: After graduation I joined a financial company, where I em-braced the concept of friendly competition and positioned myself as the go-to person for the office. Soon, I was charged with managing five associates.

Question 123. Tell me about a time when your hard work was rewarded.

SITUATION: When I worked as a legal assistant for a securities-claim law firm, I made it a point to tackle initiatives that did not fall within my job description.

ACTION: Specifically, I managed the client database, instituting up-grades and spearheading software improvement efforts to streamline processes.

RESULT: I earned a reputation as a diligent, attentive team player, and within four months of my hire, I assumed docket management activities, an unprecedented feat for the law firm.

Question 124. Give me an example of a time when you took on a task that was not part of your job description.

SITUATION: Though Mao Electronics had solid marketing and public relations departments, all the products we sold were technical in nature. Be-cause of this, neither department had the technical expertise to create mar-keting collateral.

ACTION: To assist in the marketing efforts, I offered to provide interviews to technical publications regarding the new products and our design philosophy. In addition, I wrote how-to articles for trade publications that focused on the introduction of new products.

RESULT: After the interviews and the first articles were published, the sales department reported a spike in sales.

Question 125. Tell me about a situation that called upon your strongest quality. What was the result?

SITUATION: My strongest quality is as a change agent, whereby I pinpoint operational inefficiencies and execute policies to eliminate them. This quality was especially useful when I served as incoming director for the Respiratory Clinic, where my first order of business was to turn around the low patient-satisfaction numbers.

ACTION: As part of the tactical plan, I introduced the "Rounding with Purpose" method that ensured patients were visited every hour by a nurse. In addition, I readied the department for the Joint Commission on the Accreditation of Healthcare Organizations survey.

RESULT: Shortly after my changes were implemented, the number of patients who fell out of bed declined. The department also placed in the ninetieth percentile on the Perss Ganey patient-satisfaction survey.

Question 126. Recall a time when using your initiative was rewarded.

SITUATION: When I was employed with Compact Recordings, I was commended by management for my ability to analyze situations and implement strategies that helped make it a more productive workplace.

ACTION: One specific time, I took the initiative to install hardware solutions and set up desktop configurations in preparation for a flagship account.

RESULT: I received a bonus for exceeding goals and five stars in all core competencies areas outlined in the performance evaluation.

Question 127. Describe an occasion when you created an opportunity for yourself.

SITUATION: Upon being hired by Grip Management, I noticed that the organization did not have an employee-training program.

ACTION: I had learned from my previous position at Allied Electronics of the importance of welcoming new employees with a formal company introduction. With that in mind, I created a mock workshop on PowerPoint and presented it to the department head.

RESULT: After my presentation, the company instituted a full-scale new-hire introduction program. An unexpected benefit of this plan was that turnover within the first three months of employment was reduced by 30 percent.

Question 128. Describe a time when you prepared for an obstacle in order to prevent it.

OBSTACLE: Being a consultant is a double-edged sword. Management brings me in because there are business problems that need solving, but at the same time most of them are reluctant to take the recommendations because of a fear of change, preferring to see only negatives. When Torres, Morales, and Rodriquez Law Offices brought me in to revitalize their organization, I wanted to avoid the resistance that previous clients had demonstrated to any new ideas.

ACTION: I conducted thorough client-needs assessments that asked management to reflect on changes made in the past that were unsuccessful. This approach not only gave me valuable information about the corporate culture but also gently prodded management to seriously consider my recommendations.

When I presented a new idea, I asked the attorneys for only one thing: to love the idea for fifteen minutes; during that time we discussed only the positives of the plan.

RESULT: This fifteen-minute rule kept clients' minds open enough to see the idea's advantages, and ultimately the firm agreed to implement the majority of my recommendations.

Question 129. Describe a time when you were unable to meet management expectations. What did you do about it?

OBSTACLE: I was assigned to implement a smoking cessation program at work. After putting together a comprehensive, facilitated program, I showed it to my manager. He didn't think the program would attract enough employees, and expressed interest in offering monetary incentives instead.

ACTION: I researched case studies and found that monetary incentives increase enrollment in such programs. I showed the results to my manager, and we agreed to move ahead with an incentive-based program.

RESULT: Two hundred employees joined the program, the majority quit smoking in the short term, and thirty quit for good.

Question 130. Give an example of a situation in which your greatest weakness negatively impacted a relationship or a project you were working on.

SITUATION: My e-mail communications were known to be unintentionally short and curt. Co-workers were used to my terse writing style; however, customers were not. One time, a client e-mailed me, inquiring about a new service the company had launched. In my response, I pointed her to the Web site where the features and benefits of the service were described. The client took my reply as a lack of interest in her continued business.

ACTION: Though I was able to salvage the relationship, after that incident I enrolled in an e-mail communications course to ensure that my electronic correspondences accurately reflected my intentions.

RESULT: This is a problem I am still working to correct. When I find that my e-mail messages are coming across negatively, I pick up the phone and explain.

Question 131. Recall a time when you invested time or money in developing your career.

SITUATION: I was an executive assistant at Philanthropic Enterprise for a few years, and I wanted a position in the corporate fund-raising division. Though the department had openings, the position required experience in soliciting donations. To gain experience, I approached the owner of a local animal shelter and offered to launch a pro bono event to raise money. He readily agreed to the idea.

ACTION: During my lunchtime, after work, and on weekends, I networked with people from the local chamber of commerce to secure sponsors and a location for the event. I also contacted local newspapers to provide publicity.

RESULT: The event raised $2,800 for the shelter. When another position at Philanthropic Enterprise opened up, I leveraged my experience during an internal job interview and received the promotion.

Chapter 9

Competency #4 — Analytical Skills

Challenges often arise during your typical workday, and the way you handle those problems and difficult situations determines their outcome, of course, but it also speaks volumes about how you think and act as an employee. Positive results reflect your ability to objectively assess the circumstances and decide how to close the gap between problem and solution. On the flip side, negative results demonstrate your inconsistent and unpredictable behavior—traits that ultimately hinder an organization's growth, not to mention your career growth.

An interviewer will use competency-based questions to assess your problem-solving skills and your attention to detail—in short, whether you can use a reasoned approach to solving problems and follow through on the details.

Problem Solving

Every position requires the use of problem-solving skills. Interviewers will be interested in the way you approach resolving issues, and if your methods mesh with the organization's culture.

Career Values and Behaviors

A. **Remains cool under pressure.** Does not get overwhelmed by problems; analyzes a situation and comes up with viable solutions.

Example: _____

_____

_____

B. **An astute troubleshooter.** Eliminates potential sources of problems and investigates underlying causes.

Example: _____

_____

_____

C. **Forward thinker.** Anticipates situations and proactively takes steps to mitigate risks.

Example: _____

_____

_____

D. **Innovator.** Develops creative ideas that result in sustainable changes for the organization.

Example: _____

_____

_____

E. **Reasonable.** Leaves emotions at the doorstep and tackles problems objectively, with a business perspective.

Example: _____

_____

_____

F. **Critical thinker.** Poses questions that open up discussion and weighs options to figure out solutions.

Example: _____

_____

_____

G. **Open-minded.** Lets go of preconceptions and is receptive to new ways of thinking; comes up with different approaches to a situation.

Example: _____

_____

_____

H. **Self-confident.** Confident in the possibility of achieving success, sure of one's ability to manage problems.

Example: _____

_____

_____

I. **Evaluative.** Judges situations carefully and assesses options before settling on a resolution.

Example: _____

_____

_____

J. **Intuitive.** Supplements reason with gut impressions; uses past experiences and impressions for insights into new problems.

Example: _____

_____

_____

Interview Questions and Answers

Question 132. Tell me about a time when you disagreed with management's decision. What did you do about it?

OBSTACLE: Twin Mountains encourages a collaborative environment where teams work together to prepare key account presentations. We received word from management that not everyone on the team could attend the pitch meeting because funds for travel were low. Since the clients expect senior staff to attend these meetings, that meant the production assistants could not.

ACTION: The production assistant on a special account worked just as hard, if not harder, than others in the group. I conveyed my misgivings about not inviting him, but management remained firm in its decision.

RESULT: It is important for employees, no matter their status in the organization, to feel valued. Since the assistant could not attend, I videoconferenced him in. It was a happy solution that satisfied everyone.

Question 133. Recall a time when you discovered a way to improve upon an existing process.

SITUATION: SuperMart outsourced their company's helpdesk work to Technology Solutions, my previous employer. Since it was our first multimillion-dollar account, we strived to provide exceptional service and to run the project with zero error.

ACTION: Based on my reputation for getting things done, I was selected as project leader. My accountability included rewriting the training manual to ensure that the modules focused on both hard skills, such as network troubleshooting, and soft skills, like time management and communications. After completion of the guide, I chose the technicians who would join me, and I trained them on executing the new protocols with care.

RESULT: SuperMart employees completed a survey to determine the level of service they received when contacting the helpdesk for support. We exceeded expectations and received high marks for exemplary end-user support.

Question 134. Describe a time when you figured out a problem that others had tried to solve but failed.

SITUATION: The Central Hospital emergency room had a problem with overcrowding. In the past, management disciplined the intake coordinators for not working faster. Unfortunately, though there was meeting after meeting about this, the situation did not change.

ACTION: I believed that the intake coordinators were overworked, and they were doing well, considering the resources available to them. To build upon their skills, I suggested that the IT department begin developing a patient-management software system that would allow the process to run smoother and faster.

RESULT: The software solution slashed thirty minutes off patient-processing times. An added benefit was that the buzz in the community about the shorter wait time built greater local support and enhanced the reputation for the facility.

Question 135. Give me an example about a time when a routine procedure presented a challenge.

SITUATION: One of my responsibilities with Minerals Title Company was to run in-depth title searches. To gather the information needed for clearances, I visited courthouses, tax appraisal offices, county clerk offices, and abstract offices. Most of the time the information was easy to find. However, sometimes there were discrepancies regarding who owned the property and further research was required.

ACTION: One specific title search was especially complicated and I conducted Internet searches to track down public and private information on ownership. Identifying the correct owner was more difficult than usual because the property had been handed down from generation to generation.

RESULT: My persistence paid off, and I identified the rightful owners. In fact, in the three years that I was a title searcher, I always managed to identify the property owner without resorting to soliciting help from a peer in the office.

Question 136. Describe a time when you stumbled on a problem you did not know existed.

SITUATION: My employment with MRI Technologies ranged from being so busy that taking a lunch break was impossible to being so quiet that the day was boring.

ACTION: During the downtimes, I did not spend my time browsing the Internet for the latest gadgets. Instead, I spoke with department heads to discover ways that I could improve our processes.

RESULT: It came to my attention that the problem of multiple data-entry errors needed to be addressed. After careful research, I oversaw the selection and deployment of an RIS-integrated PACs system that, in the end, slashed entry mistakes by 95 percent.

Question 137. Describe a time when you solved a problem using a skill you acquired through professional training.

SITUATION: The last training I received was on leadership, where I learned the power of attentive listening and compromise. Before training, I would have developed a plan and then delegated the responsibilities without requesting input from the team.

ACTION: Now, I choose certain projects and I ask team members for their thoughts on how to proceed in accomplishing them.

RESULT: I realized that, when given a chance, everyone in the group wants to contribute innovative ideas. Additionally, I found that when employees have a say, they take an active interest in achieving the end result.

Question 138. Tell me about an occasion when you solved a problem without using the resources you needed.

SITUATION: Along with four other people, I was hired to start a customer service department.

ACTION: As a team, we set up protocols and scripts that outlined common customer inquires. The department was coming together well, until two team members resigned within days of each other.

RESULT: Owing to a hiring freeze, neither of the ex-employees was replaced. Brenda, the remaining co-worker, and I managed to do the work of four people without increasing our hold times or sacrificing customer satisfaction.

Question 139. There are many people applying for this position. Recall the last achievement that demonstrates you are the right candidate for this position.

SITUATION: At Sports Action Company, I conceptualized, launched, and managed an active-lifestyle product line across three categories.

ACTION: Keeping in mind the company brand and its apparel program, I created advertising strategies and campaigns.

RESULT: My efforts garnered the interest of ActiveFit, the largest independent retailer for sports apparel. Securing that major account opened doors to additional lucrative contracts.

Question 140. Describe an occasion when you had to go to work sick. What were the circumstances?

SITUATION: One day, I woke up without a voice and with a slight fever. As a paralegal, I knew my presence at work was always essential but that day especially I had to prepare a report for one of the attorneys, who needed it the following day.

ACTION: Without hesitation I went into work. Unable to speak, I asked another assistant to answer my phone calls and redirect them or take messages. I focused my efforts on completing the report.

RESULT: The next day I woke up feeling worse and did not make it into work, but the attorney had the report in hand for his court date.

Question 141. Give an example of a small project that you executed that had a departmental impact.

SITUATION: As a seasoned sales manager, I was comfortable serving as mentor, coach, and motivator for the sales teams of King Red Manufacturing. Though the company's sales were strong, there was always room for improvement.

ACTION: Following a series of assessments, I lined up sales representatives with vertical markets that matched their talents, strengths, and personalities.

RESULT: This minor adjustment in territories unexpectedly netted the company an additional 8 percent in revenue.

Question 142. Describe a time when your analytical skills were put to the test.

SITUATION: As a relationship officer for Drummond Financial, I expanded the bank's relationships with its customers by acting as a consultant when offering advice on products.

ACTION: To minimize identity theft, money laundering, and terrorist financing, I complied with the USA Patriot Act and implemented "Know Your

Customer" initiatives. I always took the extra step to ask follow-up questions when a statement the client made didn't mesh with earlier comments or with completed paperwork.

RESULT: The paperwork I submitted was virtually error-free, and it was rare that a member of the quality assurance team returned any forms to me for missing information.

Question 143. Everyone's professional career is peppered with successes and failures. Describe a time when you learned from a mistake you had made.

SITUATION: I assigned a project to a team of employees. Once I outlined the expectations of the project, I left the team to their own devices as to carrying out the plan.

ACTION: When I requested an update, I was informed that the team members were at a standstill. In fact, they did not know how to get started.

RESULT: I called an emergency meeting to describe the steps they needed to take. The next time I assigned a team project, I provided guidance from the onset, to avoid uncertainty on the part of the staff.

Question 144. Describe a time when you were creative in cutting costs.

SITUATION: The real estate industry is tradition-bound. To generate interest in properties, agents usually run advertisements in newspapers, host open houses, and participate in multiple listing services. Although these are effective strategies, I wanted to use technology to reach buyers and renters.

ACTION: To expand my reach while cutting costs, I used new initiatives such as e-mailing existing and potential customers the promotional materials for open listings.

RESULT: I was successful in coordinating fifty finished leases, plus up to seven new appointments per week with clients to discuss housing needs and expectations.

Question 145. Give an example of a time when you had a positive effect on a chronic problem.

SITUATION: When I was hired as a guidance counselor for Kramer High School, the dropout rate for the school was one of the highest in the district.

ACTION: To promote the welfare of students, I counseled students concerning their academic goals, occupational preferences, and educational objectives. In addition, I evaluated transcripts to make certain students were on track to graduate on time.

RESULT: Single-handedly, I reduced the dropout rate by 28 percent, and I increased the number of students who went on to college.

Question 146. Tell me about a time when you managed more than one project at once.

SITUATION: Working for Corel, I directed and implemented over one hundred projects in six months.

ACTION: To ensure progress, I led virtual teams through the project life-cycle, including set-up and execution of schedules, test plans, contract negotiations, and systems reconfiguration while also coordinating the resources and change control in a matrix environment.

RESULT: Without exception, I delivered results within specified time schedules, within budget, and meeting quality standards and code compliance.

Attention to Detail

Time and money are lost when an employee doesn't pay attention to the details of a project he is working on. For this reason, interviewers will tap into your ability in submitting error-free work.

Key Behaviors and Career Values

A. **Thorough**. Completes projects carefully, without introducing errors.

Example: _____

_____

_____

B. **Methodical.** Takes a step-by-step approach, breaking down problems or processes into smaller portions and analyzing each.

Example: _____

_____

_____

C. **Big-picture person.** Has an ability to look at the overall picture while not neglecting the particulars.

Example: _____

_____

_____

D. **Analyzes numbers.** Scrutinizes data and evaluates sources.

Example: _____

_____

_____

E. **Pioneers new methods.** Uses innovative methods to resolve problems or cope with setbacks.

Example: _____

_____

_____

F. **Evaluates information.** Gathers and reviews data in order to draw conclusions.

Example: _____

_____

_____

G. **Diligent.** Complies with company procedures, state and federal laws, and ethical standards.

Example: _____

_____

_____

H. **Safety conscious.** Assesses environmental or safety risk factors to ensure employee protection.

Example: _____

_____

_____

I. **Persistent.** Keeps at an assignment until finished; refuses to submit paperwork until it meets meticulous standards.

Example: _____

_____

_____

J. **Industrious.** Diligent, hardworking professional; does not cut corners to get the job done faster.

Example: _____

_____

_____

Interview Questions and Answers

Question 147. Tell me about a time when you caught a problem before it escalated.

SITUATION: When I worked for Empire Raceway, I identified weaknesses in the finance department's management. Especially, I voiced concern regarding a lack of data for financial policies. If we were to face an audit, it would show that the organization clearly was in violation of regulations.

ACTION: I suggested that we hire an outside firm to go through the books. In the meantime, I established and administered the first balanced budget that the organization had in years.

RESULT: The internal auditor created a checklist of required data entries and she returned annually to inspect the records. In addition, my annual budgets kept the organization fiscally on track.

Question 148. Describe a time when your document-management skills benefited your department.

SITUATION: To avoid assigning rentals to individuals with poor credit, it was my task as property manager for Residential Horizons to ensure that all paperwork was in order and that credentials and income sources were verified.

ACTION: For quality-assurance purposes, I personally administered the background and credit checks. When potential residents passed the review, I managed the negotiations, including rent, maintenance fees, lawn-care options, and final contracts.

RESULT: Since I began administering each aspect of the rental process, all established standards, policies, and guidelines were followed. As a result, in the five years that I worked for Residential Horizons, there were no evictions or foreclosures because of failure to pay.

Question 149. Tell me about an occasion when your attention to detail was recognized by management.

SITUATION: I was contracted by the Kinder Company to act as an assistant to a finance executive when her secretary went on maternity leave.

ACTION: Part of my responsibilities was to manage the accounting and investment activities for high-net-worth clients. Since the clients had large sums of money invested in the market, they expected insightful analyses of complex data and accurate financial reports.

RESULT: Because I placed an uncompromising focus on satisfying clients' needs, I was asked to stay on as a permanent employee when the secretary decided to remain at home to raise her child.

Question 150. Describe a time when addressing a minor project detail made a significant difference in the outcome.

SITUATION: At Allied Electronics, there were a lot of calls to the support center because customers could not follow the guidelines in the various manuals and in the on-line help pages. As a technical writer, I was assigned to rewrite these documents, including the on-line help channel.

ACTION: To make the content more instructive as well as more interesting, I incorporated illustrations that supplemented the written descriptions. When finished, I also provided a final quality-assurance check for all of the new documents.

RESULT: The volume of customer calls for tech support decreased significantly. Because of the success of my efforts, management asked that I redo all other existing manuals. When the revisions were published, I received word that the new guides were all well received by customers.

Question 151. Recall a time when a thorough evaluation of events was critical to your company's success.

SITUATION: As part of a pilot program for Red Door Partnerships, I was hired as a telephone health management nurse, and I was to provide patient tele-care for clients of sixteen insurance companies with long-term healthcare policies.

ACTION: Since these services are provided over the phone, I took great care to review each patient's medications, with the objective of limiting unnecessary doctors' appointments.

RESULT: The pilot program was successful and became a full-fledged service, which saved the organizations millions of dollars in excessive medical claims.

Question 152. Give an example of a problem you solved with an obvious solution that was overlooked by others.

SITUATION: The quality of job applicants my previous employer attracted did not meet the expectations of management, largely because the company wanted to hire personnel immediately and never took the time to put best hiring practices into place.

ACTION: Since there was no official human resources department, I took the initiative of standardizing the hiring practices. I instituted background checks and drug testing as part of the screening process, as well.

RESULT: Those initiatives increased the number of qualified candidates, and thus the pool of poor hires decreased significantly.

Question 153. Tell me about an occasion when your precision was important in your work.

SITUATION: As a legal interpreter, it is my job to accurately translate every word that clients use in their statements in court. There are different dialects in Spanish, and it is important that I familiarize myself with current slang in each ethnic community.

ACTION: To gain this knowledge, I posted flyers in a nearby Hispanic community, advertising my need for a tutor.

RESULT: Since I am fluent in Spanish, a few lessons taught me the common contemporary phrases used by Mexicans and Salvadorians. In no time, I was capable of providing accurate translations of events.

Question 154. Describe a time when the attention you gave to your work led to additional responsibility.

SITUATION: Cash Cow Casino had strict guidelines for table-game supervisors. Not only were we responsible for supervising the dealers and observing the action at the tables, we were also charged with accurately completing IRS forms for proceeds generated from play in the pit.

ACTION: After my shift was over, I took care to ensure that the financial information I provided was accurate.

RESULT: My paperwork was flawless, consistently passing all internal and external audits. Management was so impressed that I was charged with training other table-game supervisors.

Question 155. Describe an occasion when you worked on a project that had little room for error.

SITUATION: When I was an architect for Structural Designs, I led the project to build an eight-story, three-hundred-office complex in the town's industrial park.

ACTION: I drew up plans with the client's vision in mind, ensuring that the structure would be aesthetically pleasing and functionally sound. In addition, I prepared scale drawings and provided spatial requirements to the contractor. Before the construction started, I made certain everything was in order, including the necessary permits.

RESULT: As an effective analyst, problem solver, and communicator, I built a solid relationship with the team members, and we met time, budget, and quality objectives.

Question 156. Give an example of a time when you went beyond standard operating procedures to ensure that regulatory compliances were met.

SITUATION: When you are dealing with HAZMAT material, it is vital that employees understand safety protocols and wear protective clothing.

ACTION: Though usually only managers take the Certified Hazardous Materials certification course, our production plant had a high incidence of injuries. As a result, I also asked employees who met the certification requirements to complete the course and take the test.

RESULT: With the knowledge gained during the certification process, these managers and employees became more diligent about following procedures. Consequently, there were fewer workers compensation claims.

Question 157. Our slogan is "Better Quality, Better Entertainment." With that in mind, give an example of a time when you served that slogan in your previous (existing) position.

SITUATION: As an assistant to a filmmaker, I was to scout locations for a documentary film; the film's subject did not want the movie to be filmed in her home.

ACTION: I took pictures of her residence to use as a reference when searching for a location. This ensured that I found a place closest aesthetically to hers.

RESULT: The subject and the filmmaker were pleased with the shoot location. Each said that I located a place with the charm and realism of the original home.

Question 158. Tell me about a time when you analyzed a situation and found many mistakes had been made.

SITUATION: I was an investigator for the forgery department of Universal Bank, and it was my job to identify fraudulent transactions. When conducting an internal audit, I realized that a significant number of flagged files had never been scrutinized.

ACTION: I contacted the customers involved to ask follow-up questions regarding their transactions. In addition, I phoned other financial institutions to find the answers to related questions.

RESULT: My efforts reduced fraudulent losses by 35 percent.

Question 159. Recall a situation in which you used more than one skill at a time.

SITUATION: As a store detective for Redline Fashion, one of my responsibilities was to apprehend customers who stole items. A group of teenagers had been banned from the premises because they had been caught swiping t-shirts. They showed up a few months later and attempted to steal electronic gadgets, but were caught again.

ACTION: I detained the guilty parties, questioned them regarding the illegal activity, and spoke with their parents and the police department, as well as testified in court.

RESULT: To ensure the court proceedings went in our favor, I completed all the paperwork with care. In addition, my good communications skills ensured that the legal process went smoothly.

Question 160. Give an example of a time when you participated in a team effort to complete a one-of-a-kind project.

SITUATION: My daily responsibility as a telephone help-desk representative was to support over two hundred users, answering their technology-related questions when they called in. As part of a special relocation project, the help desk team was tasked with reassembling the call center equipment in a newly bought building.

ACTION: I was charged with moving the hardware, installing wireless equipment, and integrating the phone system.

RESULT: Working together as a team, we made the move easier and were able to set up equipment so we would be most comfortable and efficient.

10

Competency #5— People Skills

Your understanding of people and what motivates them is a powerful attribute in the business world. "People skills" is a vague term that covers a broad range of interpersonal abilities, including how you treat others and how you expect to be treated. But it hinges on one very important talent—the ability to communicate well, whether you are buying and selling goods and services, or solving problems, or serving your fellow man.

For instance, knowing how to adjust your communication style to suit the personalities of customers or co-workers is an asset that interviewers will be looking for, especially through competency-based questions. So, how you react to the interviewer also will heavily influence that person's perception of your adaptability in the workplace. And being flexible is especially important in a global economy in which customers, clients, and business associates have many choices with whom to do business. The more pleasant you are to deal with, the more interest others will have in conducting business with you and the more benefit you will bring to the company you represent.

The fifth core competency is people skills, and those include a team orientation, an interest in customer service, and solid communications skills.

Team Orientation

Given that strong people skills are a basic ingredient of successful team-work, interviewers will ask questions that reveal the following behaviors and values.

Key Behaviors and Career Values

A. **Cooperative.** Appreciates the importance of working with others to achieve a common goal.

Example: _____

_____

_____

B. **Actively participates.** Contributes individual ideas and/or adds to team members' thoughts, so the group can come up with viable solutions.

Example: _____

_____

_____

C. **Does his/her share.** Works independently to accomplish an individual portion of the job, but keeps the team goal in mind.

Example: _____

_____

_____

D. **Understands the company's mission.** Transforms personal behavior into a professional commitment that reflects the company's goals.

Example: _____

_____

_____

E. **Shares with others.** Is a valued member of the team, sought out for opinions and information, which is openly shared.

Example: _____

_____

_____

F. **Creative.** Generates new ideas and /or improves existing ones, contributing to the team's overall success.

Example: _____

_____

_____

G. **Inspires others.** Urges team members to excel, with a keen understanding of team morale and departmental goals.

Example: _____

_____

_____

H. **Enthusiastic.** Has enviable energy levels and a can-do attitude, which are conveyed to the rest of the team.

Example: _____

_____

_____

I. **Open-minded.** Receptive to others' ideas and readily accepts constructive feedback.

Example: _____

_____

_____

J. **Trustworthy and trusting.** Both someone the team members can count on and also someone who trusts the others to meet their obligations.

Example: _____

_____

_____

Interview Questions and Answers

Question 161. Tell me about a situation in which you became aware of a serious mistake made by a colleague and what you did about it.

SITUATION: A colleague uploaded a copyrighted article to the company's intranet site.

ACTION: Through an e-mail message, I informed her that she needed to acquire permission from the copyright owner of the article. Otherwise we would be in violation of federal law.

RESULT: Since the material was online for only a few hours, she was able to remove the article without consequence. Ultimately, she received permission to reprint it and reloaded the article onto the site.

Question 162. Describe an occasion when you believed in your company even when team members had lowered morale.

SITUATION: Sunrise Nursing Home implemented a hiring freeze and all remaining employees were required to arrive earlier and leave later. Many resigned their positions in search of less stressful situations. Though I understood management's reasoning, I grew to love the residents in the nursing home. In addition, the home was ranked number three in the country, well known for its excellent programs. I took great pride in my work with the community members, so I decided to weather the storm and continue working there.

ACTION: Without protesting, I did what was asked, including taking on double shifts when necessary.

RESULT: The hiring freeze lasted well over a year, but staying on enabled me to build on that loyalty with management while also enjoying my good rapport with the residents.

Question 163. Describe a time when you were assigned a job-related task that you questioned.

SITUATION: It was hurricane season in Florida, and though a statewide evacuation was called, I was required to report to work the day of an expected hurricane. In addition, I was mandated to sleep on the premises. I had family obligations, and I was concerned that something might happen to them while I was at work.

ACTION: That said, I understood that part of my responsibility as utility engineer was to manage outages. As a result, I never shared my concerns with my manager.

RESULT: Instead, when the lights went out, I focused my efforts on getting the town's power grid up and running, so the community could go back to normal as soon as possible.

Question 164. Tell me about a time when another department's participation in a project depended on your completing a task first.

SITUATION: Since it takes time and resources to bring a project to market, it is my responsibility with the Chess Corporation to determine whether products are viable before production even begins.

ACTION: I conducted field research and participated in data collection, including analyzing market activity for similar products.

RESULT: After I made my findings, I advised corporate of consumer demands and market trends. In addition, I outlined the product specifications so the marketing department can develop campaigns.

Question 165. Describe a time when your team's effort did not meet your expectations.

SITUATION: At Coral Gables, I was part of a team charged with developing a brand strategy for an established business that was having difficulty targeting its market. Our department meetings were unorganized. No one listened to others' points of view. As such, the project was taking longer than expected.

ACTION: With the deadline approaching, everyone was working late. Though I do not mind working late, and often do, I knew that if we had come together as a team sooner, the project would have gone smoother and the deadline met without overtime.

RESULT: As a result of that experience, when I work on a project that requires a team effort, I choose my battles carefully and frequently search for a compromise that will get the project moving.

Question 166. Describe an occasion when you took direction from someone who was not your supervisor.

Situation: When I began working for Martino Public Relations firm, I was green. Without much experience, I was charged with creating a press release for one of our clients in the legal field. I was having difficulty developing a newsworthy angle.

Action: I sketched two ideas. Since I am always open to constructive feedback from colleagues, I ran my thoughts by a team member in the cubicle next to mine.

Result: He offered pointers on ways I could improve upon what I had generated. His advice was on target, and I made the necessary changes. Ultimately, the press release was picked up by the Associated Press and distributed to newspapers across the country.

Question 167. Recall a time when you had a difficult coworker as part of your team.

Situation: When I worked for the Gambini Company, I was assigned a co-worker who had a reputation for taking over projects and getting upset when her ideas were not implemented.

Action: I made a conscious decision to be sure our time together was productive. When one of her ideas had merit, but needed tweaking, I acknowledged the strength of her position before making suggestions of my own.

Result: Though it was initially difficult for her to accept another point of view, she eventually started to entertain my ideas. We put together a proposal that won the company a lucrative contract. And because we eventually got along so well, we agreed to partner on additional projects.

Question 168. Tell me about a time you worked on a project when your role was not clearly defined.

Situation: At the Century Company, a group of us were selected to participate in a beta project for the computer networking system. The project outline was not clearly defined and no one in the group knew his or her role.

Action: At the first meeting, I asked team members to describe their strengths and weaknesses. I began to list each on the dry board.

Result: Taking the role of facilitator, I encouraged everyone to choose a task based on individual interest and strengths. In no time, we had a list of priorities and everyone chose tasks that best suited their abilities.

Question 169. Give an example of a situation in your current (past) position in which you adapted to the team environment.

SITUATION: The RegPro Company prides itself on its team environment—so much so that all projects are completed as a team. This situation was new to me; in previous positions I worked independently the majority of the time. At first, I was hesitant to contribute, and for the most part I remained silent during meetings.

ACTION: After a while, I came out of my shell. I prepared talking points before the meetings that outlined my ideas for how to proceed with new and existing projects. Since I put my thoughts in order, everyone took note of my ideas.

RESULTS: Working in a team environment, in which the focus is on achieving specific goals and targets, has been a rewarding experience for me. Partnering with others has helped me hone my skills and refine the way I present ideas and interact with colleagues.

Question 170. Describe a time you took on a task that was outside the scope of your job description.

SITUATION: When I worked for Silence Alarms, the receptionist wanted to attend a training program. She was given the go-ahead as long as she found a co-worker to answer the phone while she was away.

ACTION: Because I knew that the training was important to her, I volunteered to handle the phones while she attended the seminar.

RESULT: She was grateful to me, and the day after the training, she left cookies on my desk as a thank-you. It was a lovely gesture.

Question 171. Describe a time when you worked on a project that was delayed through no fault of your own. How did you manage the situation?

SITUATION: As part of their rebranding, Buena Vista Inn hired us, Candid Solutions, to install a new light scheme for the outsides of their hotels. As part of the project, the manager of each hotel had to complete an internal survey before the lighting installation could begin. Unfortunately, though I was ready to execute the project, the majority of managers failed the survey requirements. This led to unexpected delays.

ACTION: There was nothing I could do to expedite the situation. This was a Buena Vista internal problem that I had no way of controlling. However, I met with the executives and offered to waive the lateness surcharge.

RESULT: After several months' delay, this $20 million project was underway and within budgetary requirements.

Question 172. Recall a time when you avoided getting involved in office politics.

SITUATION: Two associates applied for a management position that opened up at The Times. Michael, who had vast more experience, was chosen to head the team. Unfortunately, Tom, who had a solid track record as well, became resentful. Both of them would snap at each other at the merest opportunity. In addition, each spoke negatively about one another to others. Just about everyone in the department was forced to choose a side.

ACTION: I decided to not participate in the politicking. I was hired to manage accounts, not to fan the flames of an office dispute.

RESULT: I do not know how Michael and Tom resolved their differences. However, after a few months, the situation dissipated.

Question 173. Tell me about a time when you worked with someone who had a delicate ego.

SITUATION: I worked with an older gentleman who believed he was facing age discrimination. Whenever he was passed over for a promotion, or not assigned a challenging project, he became upset. It got to the point that when I, or anyone for that matter, did not fall in love with one of his ideas, he would get belligerent.

ACTION: To make him feel valued and respected, I befriended him. We went to lunch together a few times, and I made a point of asking about his grandchildren, whom he adored.

RESULT: Over time his hard shell softened. He came to realize that whatever problem management had with him, I did not share those sentiments.

Customer Service

Acquiring and retaining high customer-service levels adds to the vitality of an organization. Through customer-service-oriented questions, interviewers will examine how much you value consumers.

Key Behaviors and Career Values

A. **Problem resolution.** Researches procedures and processes to determine sources of problems and then finds resolutions to them; manages customer concerns.

Example: _____

_____

_____

B. **Strong follow-through.** Follows up on customer inquiries or complaints in a reasonable amount of time and corrects any problems.

Example: _____

_____

_____

C. **Customer satisfaction.** Creates an environment that encourages customers to return, with consistently positive word-of-mouth advertising.

Example: _____

_____

_____

D. **Liaison.** Effectively acts as a liaison between the sales department and the customer, to cultivate a loyal customer base that is steadily increasing.

Example: _____

_____

_____

E. **Flexible communication style.** Varies the perspective and communication style to suit the situation and ensure successful completion of assignments.

Example: _____

_____

_____

F. **Nurtures.** Regardless of a customer's attitude, approaches each situation with patience and professionalism, with the goal of gaining customer loyalty.

Example: _____

_____

_____

G. **Resourceful.** Fully understands the company's products and services, and is able to call up the information customers need to make an educated buy.

Example: _____

_____

_____

H. **Interpersonal skills.** Deals effectively with difficult customers, reserving judgment and listening to their complaints; conveys confidence and assurance.

Example: _____

_____

_____

I. **Integrity.** Readily admits mistakes or oversights and takes action to rectify the situation; conveys honesty and respect for others.

Example: _____

_____

_____

J. **Responsible.** Makes good on promises to meet or exceed customer expectations.

Example: _____

_____

_____

Interview Questions and Answers

Question 174. Describe the steps you take to ensure a high level of customer satisfaction.

SITUATION: As a bank relationship manager, it is my responsibility to build customer trust and loyalty.

ACTION: I allocate a majority of my time to educating customers on new and existing products. Because I take the time to get to know every customer and his or her goals, the majority of my clients are willing to listen to the features and benefits of my recommendations.

RESULT: I go well over my quota every month, successfully opening accounts, including custody, demand deposit accounts, and CDs.

Question 175. Describe a time when existing policies did not solve a customer's problem and the customer took his or her business elsewhere.

SITUATION: The policy at Mordancies Boutique limited the number of days that items could be returned to thirty. A customer bought a shirt to take on a three-month vacation; when she returned, she attempted to get a refund.

ACTION: I sympathized with her situation, and spoke with a manager to see if there was a way to override the company policy.

RESULT: The manager decided not to go against policy, and it was up to me to tell the customer. She was not satisfied with the outcome and she took her future business elsewhere. It is unfortunate how the relationship ended; however, I took the proper steps to manage the situation and followed company guidelines.

Question 176. As much as we may try to keep customers satisfied, there are times when we drop the ball and they are dissatisfied. Describe a time when a customer had a problem with how you managed his or her account.

SITUATION: As the shipping clerk for Direct Merchants, I was responsible for informing clients when orders were delayed, mostly because of computer glitches. I thought that I called every customer, but one time I forgot to call a long-term client. She called to inquire about her purchase, and did not take too kindly to hearing the news about the postponed shipment.

ACTION: I took full responsibility for my oversight and promised that her products would ship first thing in the morning.

RESULT: She was surprised that I did not make excuses and she commended me for not passing the buck. From that moment forward, any time she placed an order she asked for me to manage the shipment.

Question 177. Tell me about your most memorable customer-service experience. What were the circumstances?

SITUATION: When I was a patient advocate at St. Mary's Memorial Hospital, I assisted a wonderful woman who came into the hospital for heart surgery. She was scared and had no family to help her through the crisis.

ACTION: The hospital had a shortage of volunteers. I took the liberty of calling a local community center to ask whether there was someone who could visit her at the hospital.

RESULT: The next day, two volunteers showed up with books and games in hand. They helped the patient take her mind off her troubles. The doctors indicated that her good spirits assisted in her speedy recovery.

Question 178. Recall the last time a client was dissatisfied with your customer service.

SITUATION: I was going to be at an all-day training session and forgot to change my voice mail to reflect that. When I returned to the office, there were five messages from a prospect who needed information about our product line. By the last message, I could tell from the tone of her voice that she was agitated.

ACTION: I called her immediately and was not able to reach her. Then I e-mailed a quick note explaining the situation and gave her my private cell-phone number.

RESULT: When we finally communicated, she still seemed put off. She was distant on the phone, and I knew I had to resell her on our products. Understanding that she had a reason to be upset, I did not become defensive and I responded to her concerns respectfully. Ultimately, her company decided to go with another vendor, but she did e-mail me to let me know that she appreciated my professionalism and that she would keep the company in mind for future purchases. Three months later, she called again and I was able to close the deal on another service.

Question 179. Describe a position in which you used technology in answering customer inquiries. What was the process?

SITUATION: At Revolving Door Company, we sell elevator door equipment, including car enclosures, car doors and gates, and entrance frames.

ACTION: To expedite purchases and shipments, clients are required to log onto the company Web site and complete an online form that requests the purchase order number. Instantly, I receive e-mail notification, then I begin the process of tracking down the order.

RESULT: Usually the product is en route, and I notify the customer via e-mail of my findings. With the experience I gained at the Revolving Door Company, I am comfortable working in an environment where the only client contact I have is via e-mail.

Question 180. Tell me about a specific instance in which your customer-service skills were praised.

SITUATION: As the community's manager for Cooperative Gaming, I wanted to make the Web site more interactive.

ACTION: I established an online forum. To get the forum off the ground, I created the policies, guidelines, and procedures to ensure player satisfaction and retention. In addition, I recruited volunteer moderators to enforce the rules and maintain an entertaining experience for users.

RESULT: The community grew to over one hundred thousand active users, and I received a bonus for my efforts.

Question 181. Give me an example of an occasion when a customer withheld information you needed to solve a problem. How did you handle it?

SITUATION: The Knickknack Store called for a quote on a new security system. Because we have different levels of service, I attempted to uncover the client's budget. The customer indicated that there was no budget. I realize that is a common answer customers give to avoid showing their hand.

ACTION: Since it is not in my nature to press further, I began my pitch with the most expensive system. After I described the package, I was silent to give the customer an opportunity to speak and ask questions.

RESULT: At that point, the client revealed that he was interested in specific parts of the option, but could not afford the whole package. I again asked for a budget so I could customize the system to meet his monetary requirements. With his defenses down, he readily provided his budget. And I supplied the best equipment his money could buy. With all my years in sales, I have learned to meet customers where they are and not move the process along faster than they are comfortable with.

Question 182. Describe a time when you believed a system could be improved. What actions did you take?

SITUATION: Part of my job as a hospitality coordinator is to help customers when equipment malfunctions. My office was receiving complaints from customers that, once the technician left, their problems would reoccur almost immediately.

ACTION: My solution was twofold. For the short term, I called the guests after every technician visit to ensure satisfaction. For the long term, I retrained the technicians and, when necessary, let go those who failed to perform their job properly.

RESULT: The guests appreciated my thoughtfulness and the care I provided. The repeat business the hotel received made that fact evident.

Question 183. Describe a time when you made a suggestion that improved customer relations.

SITUATION: To monitor prospect activity, I suggested the organization implement the NotifyMe software as a tool to track e-mails sent, the length of time the reader spent on reading the e-mails, and the number of times the file was opened.

ACTION: When potential clients opened my e-mails several times, I sent a follow-up e-mail inquiring whether there were additional questions I could answer. When they simply skimmed the e-mail, I placed follow-up calls instead.

RESULT: The software allowed me to virtually read prospects' minds, ultimately increasing sales and customer satisfaction.

Question 184. Recall an occasion when you questioned your ability to do your job.

SITUATION: When new management took over, the operational procedures changed almost daily as the decision makers found their footing.

ACTION: For the first two days, I allowed the uncertainty to bog me down. I did not respond to client inquiries as quickly as I was accustomed to, for fear of providing the wrong information. Then I decided that the best approach was to not make any promises, instead offering options that may be available.

RESULT: Within a month, solid policies were put into place and I resumed my work habits as normal.

Communications

Advanced communication skills encourage new and repeat business, and also enhance your professional image and reputation. Since interviewers are aware of this, they will ask questions that dive into your experience using communication skills to advance your existing or past organization's goals.

Key Behaviors and Career Values

A. **Persuasive.** Convinces others, usually by example; shapes people's attitudes; and gains the buy-in of others.

Example: _____

_____

_____

B. **Composed.** Appears self-assured; addresses conflicts swiftly and confidently, with professionalism and without engaging emotional reactions.

Example: _____

_____

_____

C. **Flexible.** Adapts a style of speaking with others that picks up on their needs and conveys ideas in terms tailored to the listener's needs.

Example: _____

_____

_____

D. **Attentive listener.** Listens carefully when someone speaks, instead of thinking about what to say next.

Example: _____

_____

_____

E. **Aware of body language.** Pays attention to others' nonverbal communications (i.e., eye contact, facial expression, gestures).

Example: _____

_____

_____

F. **Effective communicator.** Provides explanations in terms that the listener will understand, while avoiding condescension.

Example: _____

_____

_____

G. **Confident.** Presents ideas with valid assurance, without dismissing the ideas of others.

Example: _____

_____

_____

H. **Reflective.** Thinks about what has been said or done before offering a response.

Example: _____

_____

_____

I. **Rapport builder.** Feels comfortable speaking with others, regardless of station, and encourages bonding.

Example: _____

_____

_____

J. **Responsive.** Reacts to the ideas of others, especially with thoughtful consideration.

Example: _____

_____

_____

Interview Questions and Answers

Question 185. Give an example of a time when you worked with someone who had an accent.

SITUATION: The restaurant business attracts people from different countries. As the manager for Knead's Eatery, I once worked with a French chef who came to the States specifically to work for us.

ACTION: The chef was fluent in English, but at times her accent made it difficult to understand what she was saying. However, when I needed clarification, I simply asked for it. And, for that matter, so did she, since she was not familiar with American expressions.

RESULT: We got along swimmingly. The language barrier was minimal, and when a problem arose, we discussed it easily.

Question 186. Describe an occasion when your communication style got you out of a tight situation.

SITUATION: I was an assistant to the CEO of International Communications Company. My communication skills were tested every day; one day, the CEO asked me to make reservations at a restaurant that was known to have a three-month waiting list—an important client was in town and he wanted to show off.

ACTION: Knowing that the restaurant would not have a table, I called anyway, hopeful that I could persuade the maitre d' to accommodate my boss. When I wasn't successful, I called a colleague whose manager had a standing reservation at the restaurant. At first she was hesitant to broach the subject with her boss, but I was persistent; I remained respectful, but pleaded with her and she came through for me.

RESULT: The client and the CEO enjoyed a fabulous dinner. By the end of the night, the deal was locked up. That deal led to a long relationship with the client, and raised my value in the eyes of my employer.

Question 187. Recall a time when you did not communicate well. What were the results?

SITUATION: Earlier in my career, I was assigned a project for which I was given minimal direction. Because I was green in the industry, I was unsure of where to start. My manager never asked if I had questions. Even though I was in over my head, I never let on and never asked for clarification.

ACTION: I dived into the project without a clue of what to do. Because the project was on deadline, I worked on it at home, conducting research.

RESULT: I met the deadline, but only with a tremendous amount of stress. As I have matured into my career, I have come to understand that asking questions is not a sign of vulnerability. I ask questions whenever necessary.

Question 188. Describe a situation when you had to tell someone bad news.

SITUATION: When I was a manager for Process Improvements Incorporated, I had to announce the layoff of six people in my department. In my years in management, I had terminated employees for poor performance, but I never had to let people go because of a financial downswing.

ACTION: I consulted an outplacement expert, who trained me on the type of employee reactions I should expect and how I should handle each situation. We did a few role-plays and I came up with a plan for how to deliver the news.

RESULT: As difficult as it was to let employees go, I kept calm and effectively delivered the message to the displaced employees. The situation went off without a hitch.

Question 189. Tell me about a time when you used your presentation skills to influence a client.

SITUATION: As the new account representative for Ballet Fashions, I was challenged to build strategic business relationships with senior executives in the fashion industry.

ACTION: Through effective networking techniques, I landed the opportunity to present our offerings to the director of marketing for a major clothing distributor. I developed a PowerPoint presentation focusing on the features and benefits of our line.

RESULT: I walked out of the meeting with a one-year contract in hand. And I was subsequently approached by team members to assist with their presentations.

Question 190. Both written and verbal communication skills are vitally important. This position relies heavily on e-mail communication. To help me assess your experience, describe a time when your written correspondence was well received.

SITUATION: As the project manager for Alter Communications, I estimated time requirements, established deadlines, monitored milestone completion, and tracked all phases of a three-tier project.

ACTION: I wrote weekly e-mails to keep team members and management apprised of changes and I provided regular status reports.

RESULT: Management and my peers constantly commended me for the quality of my messages. Most notably, they mentioned my ability to answer all their questions in one shot so there was never a need to ask follow-up questions.

Question 191. Describe an experience in which you worked with a culturally diverse population.

SITUATION: When I was a court-appointed social worker, I had a varied client base, from children in single-parent households who acted out for attention, to those who committed crimes because of drug addiction. I understood that the world in which I grew up was vastly different from that of my clients.

ACTION: From the get-go, I made a concerted effort to establish a rapport with my clients, based on mutual respect. To create a supportive environment, I always considered my clients' ages, ethnicity, religion, and culture and tailored my solutions to their circumstances.

RESULT: Once clients understood that I was willing to meet them halfway, and to guide them in a new direction, they felt at ease and freely opened up to me.

Question 192. Give me an example of when you managed to break a communications barrier.

SITUATION: When I worked for Winter Software, management decided to open an office in India, in an effort to run the operation twenty-four hours a day, at minimal cost. At first, the concept seemed flawless. When the U.S. employees went home for the day, the overseas associates could pick up on the customer projects. As it turned out, however, there was a language barrier, and the projects came back with kinks.

ACTION: I was assigned to manage the projects that went to the India office. I knew the engineers had the capacity to do the job, and that it was just a matter of communication. I did not take anything for granted. By phone, I explained each step in detail, and asked them to repeat the instructions to be certain they had understood what I said.

RESULT: As I suspected, the engineers had the skill to execute the projects. Once they understood the scope of their responsibilities, the assignments were no longer delayed and the customers were satisfied.

Question 193. Tell me about an occasion when you were optimistic while others around you were pessimistic.

OBSTACLE: When I worked for IMD, we were sure that a long-standing government contract would automatically renew. At the last minute, the decision maker decided to sign with Areotronics, a company outside of the United States. This was a big loss for our company, one that significantly dented our bottom line. Everyone in the company was cynical. Some even feared the loss of their jobs. However, I am familiar with Areotronics' culture, its people, and the way the organization functions. Based on my intimate knowledge and the government's expectations, I knew that the contract would revert to us in due time.

ACTION: I kept in contact with the government decision maker, never mentioning the lost account. Rather, I called to keep IMD in the forefront of her mind, so when the time was right, she could offer us the contract.

RESULT: As I suspected, the transition was not easy. There were more hiccups than the government employee was comfortable with. Three months into the contract, she canceled it with Areotronics and renewed with us.

Question 194. Describe a time when you were required to write marketing copy.

SITUATION: When I worked for Recreation and Racquet Club, I was charged with implementing an integrated marketing campaign that focused on offline and online advertising.

ACTION: For the offline initiative, I wrote persuasive copy and incorporated attention-grabbing photographs for a postcard campaign that was used in a direct-mail program. And for online, I created the Web site copy that outlined the features and benefits of the Club.

RESULT: The direct mail drew in local foot traffic, while the Web page, based on hits and viewing time, proved to increase merchandise sales.

Question 195. Describe an occasion when you improved communications within your department.

SITUATION: Reactions Interchange was a small company, and the owners could not afford to hire an independent network consultant to hook up a file-sharing system.

ACTION: Though we used Outlook to manage our e-mails and appointment scheduling, I read an article in the *New York Times* that Google's e-mail system, gmail, permitted users to upload documents that others could access when on different workstations. In other words, all anyone needed was a gmail account and they could log on at their leisure, read the documents, and make recommendations.

RESULT: Since gmail is a free service, it was a cost-effective tool we could use until Reactions Interchange could afford a network system.

Question 196. Tell me about a time when you strengthened a relationship through training.

SITUATION: While employed with Widgets Incorporated, one of my main responsibilities was to maintain strong relationships with distributors.

ACTION: In an effort to sustain profitable relationships, I implemented semi-annual meetings that focused on budget evaluations, forecasts, and new-brand launchings.

RESULT: This hands-on approach enhanced distributors' performance.

Question 197. Give an example of an important written document you are required to write.

SITUATION: As a contract writer, I prepare three hundred contracts a month, with little or no interaction with customers. Almost all the information I receive comes from the sales representatives.

ACTION: When I write the official contracts, I have to take into account the legal aspects as well as any notes the sales representatives have given me.

RESULT: Since the contracts I write are known to be accurate, every salesperson requests that I work on his or her accounts.

Question 198. Recall a time when a team member criticized your work in front of others. How did you respond?

SITUATION: During a meeting, I inadvertently submitted the first draft of a report, which was missing a crucial final portion of the proposal. A colleague, Paul, pushed the report into the middle of the table, and in a snarky tone, told me it was incomplete. It was evident that the others present were uncomfortable by his approach, as the room went silent.

ACTION: I looked through the report and noticed my mistake. With calm demeanor, I excused myself to make copies of the final report.

RESULT: When I returned the meeting was under way. Without interrupting, I passed out the new report. After my presentation was complete, Paul praised the hard work I had put into it. I suspect that if I had responded negatively, or defensively, to his remark, the meeting would have turned even more uncomfortable. There are times when we have to decide *not* to react and to let things slide, for the benefit of all involved.

Question 199. Describe a time when you were praised for your listening skills.

SITUATION: As a benefits administrator, employees routinely approach me to ask questions about their life insurance. One time, an employee's spouse had passed away; she came into my office distraught, asking me to call the life insurance company for her, since she was at a loss for words.

ACTION: With her sitting in my office, I made the appropriate call to put the process of payment into action. I also took the time to listen, as she expressed her feelings about her loss.

RESULT: After the meeting, the employee thanked me for my generosity and for allowing her to voice her sorrow.

Question 200. Describe a situation in which you found yourself dealing with someone with whose personality you clashed. How did you handle the situation? What was the outcome?

OBSTACLE: While I was the co-manager of Deep Blue Salon, the shop enjoyed years of profitability, partially because we were the only place in town. As the town began to grow, new businesses emerged, including another salon within three miles of Deep Blue. My outlook was that competition is healthy. On the other hand, Tara, the other manager, was troubled by the prospect of another salon. Whereas I wanted to revise our marketing plan to gear up for a possible decrease in business, she was not open to the idea.

ACTION: After attempting to engage her in the process several times without success, I forged ahead. I devised a plan that included expanding our services to provide Reiki and stone massages.

RESULT: When I completed a draft of the new plan, I showed it to Tara. I felt that it was important to get her input before the final product. Once she reviewed the outline, she jumped on board and shared her thoughts. Together, we polished the plan, and when the new salon opened, we remained competitive.

Question 201. Tell about a time you built rapport quickly with someone under difficult conditions.

OBSTACLE: When I was hired as a project assistant for Reynolds Incorporated, the employee assigned to train me was the person I was replacing. Unfortunately, she gave her two-week notice under difficult circumstances. The first day on the job was uncomfortable for me. She did not talk to me unless it was about a work-related matter and even then she was curt.

ACTION: I understood that her animosity toward the company had nothing to do with me. To ensure a smooth transition, however, I did not react negatively to her attitude. After a day or two, her unenthusiastic approach subsided.

RESULT: By the end of the two weeks, we were having lunch together. In fact, she gave me her personal e-mail address, just in case questions arose later on.

Part III

The End of
the Interview

11

Closing the
Job Interview

The difference between landing a job offer and the employer's choosing to hire someone else could lie in your close to the interview. You've meted and greeted, and you've answered some tough questions. Now, you need to make a good exit. A simple handshake and the exchange of a few pleasantries are important—expected traditions to keep in mind. However, those are not enough to win the interviewer's consideration.

To complement these conventional practices, consider the following four strategies:

1. Find out if and when any next rounds of interviews will take place. This information will give you an opportunity to ask for an invitation to that next round. For example, "I am interested in participating in the next round. When can I expect a call for scheduling?"

2. Ask the interviewer whether you answered all the questions satisfactorily. In addition, ask outright if the interviewer has any concerns about your application. You may be hesitant about asking this, perhaps fearful of the answer, but the reality is that, if the interviewer has concerns about your qualification, you want to know what they are before you leave the meeting. This may be your only opportunity to squelch those misunderstandings and misgivings. For example, "Before we call it

a day, I would like to know if there are any more questions you have for me or perhaps any concerns about my candidacy."

3. Inquire about a date for the hiring decision. Sometimes it is only a matter of days, other times it may be weeks. Either way, you want to know so you can follow up appropriately. So ask, "By what date do you expect to make a decision?"

4. Ask interviewers for their contact information, should you need to reach them. For example, "Thank you for taking the time to meet with me today. This informative interview answered many of my questions. Should I need additional information, would you rather I contact you via e-mail or phone?"

With the above four strategies in place, you gain an edge over the other interviewees. To increase your chances of selection even further, there are interview blunders to avoid.

Some Closing Mistakes

Unfortunately, after all the hard work job seekers put into their search, including their résumés and cover letters, the networking, and the interview questions, many candidates make a wrong move at the very end that costs them the job. The following three common mistakes are easy to avoid when you know what to look for.

✔ *Mistake 1. Saying no before the job is offered.* An occasion may arise during the interview when you decide that you do not want the job. Regardless of the reason (e.g., salary, personality incompatibility, no room for growth), refrain from turning down a position before it is offered. The reason is twofold: (1) the intention of the interview is to receive a job offer. When you turn down a position prematurely, you will never know if your interview skills are up to par; and (2) interview settings are emotional situations, prone to quick and often inaccurate reactions. Your dissatisfaction with the job may be with the interview itself and not with the responsibilities of the position. Do not say no to a position before you have had the time to consider its suitability for you.

Take twenty-four hours to process the interview, comparing the company's expectations and your comfort with the position's fit; this the norm and good practice.

⊘ *Mistake 2. Apologizing for your performance.* The last words you impart should not be negative. Being apologetic will make you seem as though you lack confidence. No one wants to hire an individual who does not have pride in his or her abilities. When you apologize for your performance, you may hint at a personality characteristic that may not have been in the interviewer's mind.

However, this is not to suggest that, if there is an issue you want to bring up that will clarify a misunderstanding that occurred during the interview, that you should *not* do it. The way you approach the matter is what's important. For example, toward the end of the interview, the interviewer usually asks a question such as, "Would you like to add anything else?" If you did not answer a earlier question fully, simply state, "Upon reflection, when I answered the question _____, I should have added _____." That response is much better than what candidates usually say, which is "I do not know what I was thinking. When I answered _____, I forgot to mention _____." The difference between the two responses is significant. The first is a normal part of conversation; the second sheds a negative light on your "forgetfulness."

⊘ *Mistake 3. Broaching the subject of salary.* Interviewers are the ones who should raise the matter of compensation. When interviewers do not ask for salary requirements, it is an indication that the timing is not right. Pressing the topic before its time will cause interviewers to question your interest in the position. Or, the interviewer may low-ball your qualifications because he did not have enough information about your experience to offer an acceptable salary. Be patient. Take the interviewer's lead.

The Closing Statement

At the end of the interview, you have the opportunity to make a closing statement. Those are the last words you will utter before you leave the office, so make them count. Since there is no definitive way to close an interview, below are some options for you to consider.

✅ *Summary Close.* Provide the interviewer with a synopsis of your experience. Remember that competency-based interviews are rooted in details, so bring them up again. For example, "As a quality-focused IT professional with more than ten years of experience as a systems technician and software/hardware support specialist, I have demonstrated a proven ability to create and deliver solutions that meet corporate objectives tied to business and technology performance. I am skilled in proactively identifying and resolving critical systems/network issues that will benefit the IT department. As such, I hold a sincere interest in joining your team."

✅ *Direct Close.* If you want the job, then ask for it. For example, "Thank you for taking the time to interview me today. Based on our conversation, my background is a perfect fit with the job requirements we discussed. Given that, I am interested in joining your team."

✅ *Balance Sheet Close.* Remind the interviewer of the core competencies that were stressed during the interview and how your background is a natural fit. For example, "This interview has been informative. From our discussion, it is evident that the position requires an accounting representative with experience in processing payroll, quarterly payroll returns, and general ledger account reconciliation. As I demonstrated, I have the know-how in each category to begin working with little or no training. When can I expect to hear from you?"

✅ *Compliment Close.* Summarize the aspects of the position and/or company that intrigue you. For example, "Over the years, your organization has been the leader in laser technology. The new strides and the direction your organization is taking demonstrate a strong commitment to the field. Since I take my career seriously and have strived to be the best I can be, I would like to join your team."

✅ *Standing-Room-Only Close:* If you received an offer from another company before you went to the interview, let the interviewer know. For example, "I received a job offer yesterday and decided to interview today because your organization piqued my interest. After today's meeting, I am glad I made the decision to interview with you. This position is my first choice. When do you expect to make a hiring decision? The other employer is expecting my response by the end of the week."

☑ *Testimonial Close.* Add a compliment that you received from a customer, management, or business associate. For example, "At my last performance review, my supervisor indicated that I have superior client support skills. She noted that I successfully met the company's expectations when managing hundreds of support calls per day under strict time constraints and guidelines. I would like to bring my experience to work for your department."

☑ *Trial Close.* Offer to demonstrate your ability to perform the tasks. For example, "If it would make the decision easier, I would like to work on a trial basis to demonstrate the event planning skills I have honed over the years. You will find that my ability to manage details and execute plans and promotions will compliment your department's needs. How about I participate in an audition interview where you hire me on a probationary period so you can see me in action before you make a final decision?"

Chances are, interviewers will put emphasis on the last words you shared, so choosing a closing statement that fits your personality, the position, and the interviewer's expectations will leave a lasting impression.

There's much more to the close of a competency-based interview than simply shaking hands and saying good-bye. The end of the interview gives you one last chance to make a strong impression, to summarize why you are the right person for the job, and to correct any misconceptions that may have cropped up. You can also find out what to expect next.

Chapter **12**

The Interview Follow-Up

Sending the interviewer a follow-up letter ensures that you remain in the forefront of his or her mind. It also positions your candidacy ahead of the others, who haven't sent such a letter. Though sending a thank-you letter is a simple task, the majority of job seekers fall into the "no follow-up trap," for the following two reasons:

1. *Fear of rejection.* Worried that the answer is no, jobseekers often would rather wait it out than send a letter that will yield a negative response quicker. Most want to hold on to the hope, to the possibility of a yes. However, the sooner you know the interviewer's intentions, whether negative or positive, the better off you are, since knowing will allow you to focus your efforts on other opportunities, if need be.

2. *Do not want to appear pushy.* Most job seekers mistakenly believe that, if the interviewer is interested, he or she will call. Furthermore, a common misunderstanding is thinking that sending a letter smacks of desperation. On the contrary, the opposite is true. Following up on the interview demonstrates your unwavering enthusiasm for the position. This sentiment leads the interviewer to take your candidacy more seriously than someone else's.

A CareerBuilder.com survey, "How to Get in the Front Door," was sent to more than 650 hiring managers. The results were as follows:

- ✅ Nearly 15 percent of hiring managers reject a job candidate who neglects to send a thank-you letter after the interview.
- ✅ 32 percent said that they would still consider the thankless prospect, but that their opinion of him or her was diminished.

With statistics such as those, it is in your best interests to follow up and put aside any qualms you may have for doing so. The CareerBuilders survey also indicated that, although most hiring managers expect to receive a thank-you note, the format preferences differ. One in four hiring managers prefer to receive a thank-you note via e-mail only; 19 percent want the e-mail followed up with a hard copy; 21 percent want a typed hard copy only; and 23 percent prefer just a handwritten note.

Following-Up Pointers

The purpose of the interview is not to ask about the job. It is to express your interest in the position. With this in mind, consider the following additional pointers about handling the follow-up:

- ✅ Do not assume the worst. Depending on the number of candidates interviewed, the hiring decision can take longer than you would like. However, it is best to never assume the worst. Unless you have inside information, you will never know what is going on behind the scenes. Playing a guessing game will cause unnecessary distress.

- ✅ Keep your industry in mind when choosing to either call or send an e-mail. As an example, a salesperson's assertiveness may be acceptable, whereas for an accountant, whose profession is more laid back, assertiveness may not be welcome.

- ✅ When interviewers do not get back to you, let go. From your point of view, the interviewer should take the time to either offer you the job or let you know that another candidate was chosen. Unfortunately, interviewers dislike informing candidates of negative outcomes, for two reasons: First, when they do reach out, many candidates begin to ask questions, requesting another opportunity; some even become hostile. A phone call that should take less than a minute becomes a fifteen-minute conversation. And, second, even when the phone calls are short, multiply that by hundreds of applicants and you can see that these calls take a huge chunk out of an interviewer's day. Though it is nice to receive acknowledgment, it is easier for interviewers not to return phone calls or e-mails.

⊘ Give your thank-you letter a twist by providing additional information. Along with your letter, include an informational piece, such as an article or a Web site address that is relevant to the interview. Depending on your line of work, you can submit writing samples or graphics based on your conversation. Sending such pertinent information gives you another chance to interact with the interviewer and keep your name in the forefront. However, this step can come off as insincere, so use it only when you are truly earnest about the job.

⊘ Know when to let go. When an interviewer has decided to hire someone else, you will not change his mind, no matter how many times you call.

⊘ Stick to traditional follow-up methods. Online social networks such as Facebook or MySpace are not follow-up avenues you should use. Those methods are too informal. E-mail, a letter sent through regular mail, or a phone call are better.

⊘ Ask for a second interview. With every interview the interviewer conducts, the criteria for the position change. You may have had a great interview and raised the stakes. If you were one of the first interviewed, yours may not measure up because later candidates each brought something new to the situation. Asking for a second interview will put you back on the same playing field.

Competency-Based Follow-Up Letters

There isn't a standard follow-up letter to use as a guide. So, to determine how best to focus the letter, take the time to complete the following post-interview assessment. The results can serve as a roadmap for your approach.

The first step in the assessment is to collect your thoughts right after the interview. Write down your initial impressions while your memory is fresh. If you feel the need, share your perspective with a friend—an objective opinion may shed light on aspects you overlooked. Writing down or sharing the circumstances of the interview has a way of unclogging your thoughts.

Points to consider when evaluating an interview include the following:

1. Name the reasons you remain interested in the position.

_____

_____

_____

2. List three questions you believed you answered well.

_____

_____

_____

3. Identify five core competencies that the interviewer focused on the most.

_____

_____

_____

4. Give three reasons the interviewer may be reluctant to hire you.

_____

_____

_____

5. List the questions you would have answered differently if given another opportunity.

_____

_____

_____

6. Did you deliver the key points you wanted to get across?

_____

_____

_____

Once the assessment is completed, begin working on the competency-based follow-up letter. For each of the following types of letters, there is a sample that can serve as a guide when writing your own correspondence.

- ⊘ *Core Competency Focus.* Determine the top three core competencies that were stressed during the interview and write a thank-you letter that touches on each (Figure 12-1).
- ⊘ *"Story Telling" Follow-Up Letter.* Present the interviewer with a story regarding your experience (Figure 12-2).
- ⊘ *SOAR Cover Letter.* Compose a letter using the SOAR concept (described in Chapter 2). Choose three recent challenges and outline each (Figure 12-3).
- ⊘ *Listing of Core Competencies.* Simply list your proficiencies and/or personal attributes (Figures 12-4 and 12-5).
- ⊘ *Job Description Focus.* Before leaving the interview, request a copy of the job description; most interviewers are happy to oblige. Read through the job description and choose three points to expand upon in the follow-up letter (Figure 12-6 gives a sample job description, Figure 12-7 is a letter example).

Regardless of which option you choose, be sure to convey your enthusiasm for the position and for working for the hiring organization.

Figure 12-1

MARK SILVER

284 West 73rd Street
Lyford, Texas 78569
(956) 555-1212
silver@email.com

[Date]

[Name]
[Title]
[Company Name]
[Address]
[City, State, Zip]

Dear [name],

Throughout my career, the cornerstone of my success has been an ability to provide direction, operational planning, and streamline innovative technology solutions across an organization. I have developed a strong track record of synchronizing with executive management teams to create and implement improvements and cost-effective applications that enhance operations.

During the interview, I took the opportunity to showcase the core competencies that previous employers have commended me for, including:

- **Strategic Vision** – With a knack to communicate vision and institute a roadmap that shapes organizational goals and course of actions, I define future-focused objectives that boost productivity.

- **Project Management Skills** – My strong background in managing a full cycle of projects, from requirements gathering to implementation, has honed my ability to successfully execute plans.

- **Budget Administration** – As a thoughtful, yet decisive, decision-maker, I evaluate costs, anticipate challenges to mitigate risks, and administer operating budget to launch technology initiatives.

In addition, I work effectively in dynamic, challenging environments that require immediate adaptability and creative thinking. Currently, I am exploring new opportunities where I can leverage my cross-functional leadership skills and solutions-directed mind-set to meet strategic business needs.

To provide you with details concerning my qualifications and accomplishments, my resume is enclosed. I would welcome the opportunity for an interview to discuss your company's needs and the results you can expect from me. Thank you for your time and consideration.

Sincerely,

Mark Silver

Mark Silver

Figure 12-2

JUAN MELENDEZ

4932 Pentagon Drive ▪ Marietta, GA 30066 ▪ (770) 555-1212 ▪ Melendez@email.com

---

[Date]

[Name]
[Title]
[Company Name]
[Address]
[City, State, Zip]

Dear [name],

As I mentioned during the interview, treating individuals with cerebral palsy has been a passion of mine since my younger brother was diagnosed at the age of two. I have always been proud of his tenacity and his therapist's sincere interest in ensuring his growth.

We also discussed my strong ability to provide one-on-one modalities that enable me to customize a patient's therapy. Since there is not a standard practice for cerebral palsy patients, my creative approach assists patients in overcoming challenges and to live independent lives.

I take great care in reviewing a patient's file to determine his range of motion, balance coordination, and motor function. Once I implement a plan, I continuously monitor the progress and modify treatments as necessary. Patient evaluations that I receive rank in the 95th percentile for customer satisfaction.

With my dedication in serving cerebral palsy patients and the skills outlined during our interview, we are a perfect fit. I remain interested in the position. You can reach me at (770) 555-1212.

Sincerely,

Juan Melendez

Juan Melendez

Figure 12-3

Jordan Schwartz
I4 Yard Street
Madison WI
(608) 555 – 1212
swartz@email.com

[Date]

[Name]
[Title]
[Company Name]
[Address]
[City, State, Zip]

Dear [name],

As a contractor virtual assistant, it is imperative that I integrate a flexible work style to ensure that I meet the needs of various employers. As I touched upon during our meeting, I have met diverse challenges, including:

Challenge #1

Situation: ABC law firm was in the middle of preparing depositions for a class action lawsuit when the company computer crashed. Their information technology specialist informed the attorneys it would take a while to retrieve the lost information. This is when it was decided to hire a Virtual Assistant.

Action: Based on my reputation as an employee with a strong work ethic, I was selected to prepare legal documents.

Result: We were on a tight deadline and I stayed up all night to ensure the attorneys on the case received the information they needed to postmark the envelope before 5pm.

Challenge #2

Situation: The permanent secretary was on a two-week vacation and I was hired to answer the phone and perform light administrative tasks.

Action: The functions I implemented included clerical support, general office operation, and travel arrangements.

Result: For the past two years, every time the secretary goes on vacation, I am the "go-to" virtual assistant.

I appreciate the time you took to interview me. I am very interested in working for you and look forward to hearing from you about this position. Please feel free to contact me at anytime if further information is needed. My cell phone number is (555) 111-1111.

Sincerely,

Jordan Schwartz

Jordan Schwartz

Figure 12-4

Yvette McRaney

383 Abraham Road
Lake Forest, IL 60045

(847) 555-1212
yvette.mcraney@email.com

[Date]

[Name]
[Title]
[Company Name]
[Address]
[City, State, Zip]

Dear [name],

A visionary, results-proven marketing executive with track record of success in innovative strategies are the qualities I can bring to the table. With an ability to lead product branding through the full cycle, from concept development and refinement through launch, I have comprehensive experience within a broad range of situations, including start-up, turnaround, and high growth environments. Most notably, my efforts have consistently…

- Enhanced Brand Recognition
- Secured Lucrative Sponsorships
- Cultivated Strategic Relationships

- Nurtured Client Relations
- Optimized Marketing Campaigns
- Improved Segment Performance

Complementing the core competencies outlined above, my successes include the re-launch of a magazine, which played an instrumental role in the publication receiving the Henry R. Luce Award in 2008 for "editorial excellence in photography."

I would like the opportunity to join your team as a marketing executive where I can incorporate my knowledge in integrated marketing strategies. I look forward to hearing from you regarding your decision.

Sincerely,

Yvette McRaney

Yvette McRaney

Figure 12-5

Clint Anderson

837 Barley Road · Livermore, CA 94550 · (925) 555 – 1212 · clintanderson@email.com

[Date]

[Name]
[Title]
[Company Name]
[Address]
[City, State, Zip]

Dear [name],

Thank you for taking time out of your busy schedule to interview me for the second grade teacher position for the Sayville school district. Based on the discussion we had yesterday, I took the liberty of outlining the classroom management skills, manipulatives that I incorporate in the classroom, and the personal attributes that have served me well during my years as an educator.

Classroom Management Skills	Manipulative Integration	Personal Attributes
– Creative Lesson Planning	– Blocks & Clocks	– Persuasive Communicator
– Student Motivation	– Problem-solving Cards	– Dependable & Loyal
– Role Playing Exercises	– Tangram Pieces	– Creative Thinker

In addition to the aforementioned skills, I have comprehensive experience in successfully meeting the educational needs of all students by developing curriculum materials that provide both individualized and small group instruction. As part of an integrated effort, I have identified students' needs and cooperated with support staff in assessing and helping students solve health, attitude, and learning problems.

Should you have additional questions before a final decision is made, you can contact me at the email and phone number indicated above. In the meantime, for your reference, I am enclosing copies of parent letters that I received throughout the years.

Sincerely,

Clint Anderson

Clint Anderson

Enclosure

Figure 12-6

SAMPLE JOB DESCRIPTION

Position Title: Director, Operations
Reports To: Chief Business Officer
Status: Exempt

OVERVIEW

The Operations Director is responsible for all aspects of the administration and strategic planning of the production operations for the organization. This position will analyze, design, and implement operational strategies, systems, and policies to optimize production efficiency and ensure continuous improvement and provide leadership and direction to the department and collaborate with the management team to maximize workflow and operational growth.

ESSENTIAL RESPONSIBILITES

- Responsible for the daily functions of the Operations Department.
- Manage projects and oversee administrative details.
- Formulate, budget, and assess strategic solutions of projects.
- Collaborate with project management teams.
- Develop, maintain, and effectively communicate procedural manuals.
- Analyze and prepare reports and operational documents for the department.
- Provide resources to achieve productivity to include information, equipment, and materials.
- Comply with the organization's best practices and principles.
- Adhere to safety procedures including ensuring equipment maintenance and safety gear.
- Ensure compliance with local, state, and federal standards and regulations.
- Communicate changes to the department.
- Develop plans to achieve goals, objectives, and priorities for the department.
- Supervision, recruitment, and disciplinary actions of staff.
- Coach, lead, and manage the work of direct reports.
- Administer performance evaluation and provide professional development opportunities. to subordinates.
- Evaluate and provide professional development opportunities.
- Perform other responsibilities as required or assigned.

MINIMUM EMPLOYMENT STANDARDS

- Bachelor's degree related to job functions.
- Must have a minimum of five years of related experience.
- Proven leadership and management skills, with experience in motivating staff.
- Experience in managing teams in a fast-paced environment.
- Strong project management skills and detail oriented.
- Knowledge of budget management.
- Excellent verbal and written communication skills.
- Proficient in the use of computer programs including word processing and spreadsheet applications.

Figure 12-7

COREY SANDLER

MANAGEMENT PROFESSIONAL: CLIENT SERVICES, BUSINESS
DEVELOPMENT, COMMUNICATIONS, ACCOUNT MANAGEMENT,
EMPLOYEE DEVELOPMENT, OPERATIONS

28 South Avenue
Minneapolis, MN 55408
Home: 612-555-1212
Mobile: 612-555-4863
csandler@email.com

[Date]

[Name]
[Title]
[Company Name]
[Address]
[City, State, Zip]

Dear [name],

The time you took to interview me for the director of operations position is greatly appreciated. Along with my results-driven approach, you can be assured that I would uphold the highest level of work detail and ethical standards as a member of your team. I am flexible and adaptable to both new situations and changing organizational needs.

Core Competencies Outlined in Job Description	My Experience
Manage daily functions of the Operations Department	Oversaw core business and operation development functions (e.g., purchasing, human resources, finance, quality control, material management) within manufacturing operations.
Maximize operational growth	Increased gross profit margin 17% by restructuring organization through root cause analysis and process management/JIT initiatives.
Optimize production efficiency	Improved on-time delivery from 18% to 93% within 1 year by implementing project planning system based on teamwork, quality, and customer satisfaction goals.

As you will note, I have comprehensive experience in the areas that are most important for the position. Complementing the highlighted proficiencies above is my ability to manage profit and loss performance, including monitoring group and individual project performance; preparing and administering internal budgets; and monitoring workflow practices with respect to quality, safety, and profitability.

Enclosed is a progress chart that outlines year-after-year productivity increases that my existing employer has commended me for. I would like to put years of establishing and meeting business objectives to work for Intel Communications.

Sincerely,

Corey Sandler

Corey Sandler

Contributors

A special thank-you to the following:

Beth Mann
Hot Buttered Media
http://www.hotbutteredmedia.com

Wendy S. Enelow, CCM, MRW, JCTC, CPRW
Executive Resume Writer & Career Consultant
Author of 30+ résumé, cover letter, and career books
www.wendyenelow.com

Barb Matias
Human Resources Professional

American Management Association
www.amanet.org

About the Author

Linda Matias has earned credentials in all three primary aspects of the job search: Certified Interview Coach (CIC), Job & Career Transition Coach (JCTC), and Nationally Certified Resume Writer (NCRW). Through her career and outplacement firm, CareerStrides, Linda serves as a career consultant, where she coaches professionals on changing careers and best résumé and interview strategies. As part of her career management program, she provides individual and group coaching sessions for professionals seeking a career change. Dispensing advice on topics including changing careers, résumé writing, and effective interview techniques, Linda effectively prepares her clients to move in a smooth career transition.

Solidifying her experience in the résumé writing and interview fields, Linda is the former president of the National Resume Writers' Association and the director of the Certified Interview Coach Institute. You can visit her Web site at www.careerstrides.com.

American Management Association
www.amanet.org